D1279655

Computers

**Titles in the
Discovering Careers
series**

**Adventure
Animals
Computers
Construction
Environment
Health
Math
Nature
Science
Space Exploration
Sports
Transportation**

DISCOVERING CAREERS

Computers

Ferguson's
An Infobase Learning Company

Discovering Careers: Computers

Copyright © 2011 by Infobase Learning

Ferguson
An imprint of Infobase Learning
132 West 31st Street
New York NY 10001

Library of Congress Cataloging-in-Publication Data

Computers.
        p. cm. — Discovering Careers
    Includes biographical references and index.
    ISBN-13: 987-0-8160-8049-6 (hardcover : alk. paper)
    ISBN-10: 0-8160-8049-6 (hardcover : alk. paper)   1. Computer science—Vocational guidance—Juvenile literature.

    QA76.25.C555 2011
    004—dc22

Ferguson books are available at special discounts when purchased in bulk quantities for businesses, associations, institutions, or sales promotions. Please call our Special Sales Department in New York at (212) 967-8800 or (800) 322-8755.

You can find Ferguson on the World Wide Web at http://infobasepublishing.com

Text design by Erika K. Arroyo and Erik Lindstrom
Composition by Erik Lindstrom
Cover printed by Bang Printing, Brainerd, Minn.
Date printed: March 2011
Printed in the United States of America

10 9 8 7 6 5 4 3 2 1

This book is printed on acid-free paper.

CONTENTS

Introduction

You may not have decided yet what you want to be in the future. And you don't have to decide right away. You do know that right now you are interested in computers. Do any of the statements below describe you? If so, you may want to begin thinking about what a career in computers might mean for you.

____My favorite school assignments are the ones I do on the computer.
____I spend a lot of time surfing the Internet.
____I use e-mail and text messages to talk with my friends.
____I enjoy teaching others how to use computers.
____I am good at computer games.
____I designed my own Web site.
____I like to take things apart and put them back together.
____I am interested in computer languages.
____I am interested in animation.
____I would like to learn more about how to build computers.
____I know how to do minor repairs on my computer.
____I belong to a computer club.
____I am interested in writing new software programs.
____I keep up with all the latest computer technology.

Discovering Careers: Computers is a book about careers in computers, from Computer Network Specialists to Webmasters. Technology changes so quickly that computer specialists will be in constant demand for a long time. Computers offer opportunities in developing that technology, writing new programs, exploring Internet possibilities, and managing day-to-day operations.

This book describes many possibilities for future careers that focus on computers. Read through it and see how the different careers are connected. For example, if you are interested in creating video games, you will want to read the chapter on Computer and Video Game Designers. If you would like to teach others about how to use computers, then you should read the articles on Computer Trainers or Teachers, Computer Science. If you think you would like to design computer hardware or software, you should read the articles on Computer Programmers, Graphics Programmers, Hardware Engineers, Software Designers, and Software Engineers. If you are interested in the Internet, you will want to read the chapters on Computer Security Specialists, Internet Transaction Specialists, Web Designers, and Webmasters. Go ahead and explore!

What Do Computer Specialists Do?

The first section of each chapter begins with a heading such as "What Computer Support Specialists Do" or "What Technical Writers and Editors Do." It tells what it's like to work at this job. It describes typical responsibilities and assignments. You will find out about working conditions. Which computer specialists work alone and which ones work on teams? Do they work in one location or do they travel to various locations? This section answers all these questions.

How Do I Become a Computer Specialist?

The section called "Education and Training" tells you what schooling you need for employment in each job—a high school diploma, training at a junior college, a college degree, or more. It also talks about on-the-job training that you could expect to receive after you're hired, and whether or not you must complete an apprenticeship program.

How Much Do Computer Specialists Earn?

The "Earnings" section gives the average salary figures for the job described in the chapter. These figures give you a general idea of how much money people with this job can make. Keep in mind that many people really earn more or less than the amounts given here because actual salaries depend on many different things, such as the size of the company, the location of the company, and the amount of education, training, and experience you have. Generally, but not always, bigger companies located in major cities pay more than smaller ones in smaller cities and towns, and people with more education, training, and experience earn more. Also remember that these figures are current averages. They will probably be different by the time you are ready to enter the workforce.

What Will the Future Be Like for Computer Specialists?

The "Outlook" section discusses the employment outlook for the career: whether the total number of people employed in this career will increase or decrease in the coming years and whether jobs in this field will be easy or hard to find. These predictions are based on economic conditions, the size and makeup of the population, foreign competition, and new technology. They come from the U.S. Department of Labor, professional associations, and other sources.

Keep in mind that these predictions are general statements. No one knows for sure what the future will be like. Also remember that the employment outlook is a general statement about an industry and does not necessarily apply to everyone. A determined and talented person may be able to find a job in an industry or career with the worst outlook. And a person without ambition and the proper training will find it difficult to find a job in even a booming industry or career field.

Where Can I Find More Information?

Each chapter includes a sidebar called "For More Info." It lists organizations that you can contact to find out more about the field and careers in the field. You will find names, addresses, phone numbers, e-mail addresses, and Web sites of computer-oriented associations and organizations.

Extras

Every chapter has a few extras. There are photos that show computer workers in action. There are sidebars and notes on ways to explore the field, lists of recommended personal and professional qualities, fun facts, profiles of people in the field, and lists of Web sites and books that might be helpful.

At the end of the book you will find three additional sections: "Glossary," "Browse and Learn More," and "Index." The Glossary gives brief definitions of words you may be unfamiliar with that relate to education, career training, or employment. The Browse and Learn More section lists computer-related books, periodicals, and Web sites to explore. The Index includes all the job titles mentioned in the book.

It's not too soon to think about your future. We hope you discover several possible career choices. Happy hunting!

Computer and Electronics Sales Representatives

What Computer and Electronics Sales Representatives Do

Computer and electronics sales representatives sell computer and electronics equipment to customers and businesses of all sizes. Sometimes they also install computer systems, provide maintenance, or train the client's staff. Sales representatives who work for retail stores deal with consumers. They sell computers,

EXPLORING

- Read computer magazines and newsletters, as well as blogs and online discussion groups.
- Keep up with the latest computer equipment, including hardware, software, printers, scanners, games, and digital cameras.
- Create a marketing plan for one of your favorite video games or software programs.
- Join computer clubs organized by your school or community center.

- Get a part-time job in sales—preferably at a computer or electronics store.
- Talk to a sales representative about his or her career. Ask the following questions: What made you want to enter this career? What are your main and secondary job duties? What do you like least and most about your job? How did you train for this field? What advice would you give a young person who is interested in the field?

A sales worker explains the features of various computers to a customer. (Ben Margot, AP Photo)

computer software, printers, scanners, modems, monitors, disk drives, networking cables, computer and video games, and any other component that is needed to use a computer or that a customer may wish to add. Sales representatives who specialize in a particular piece of hardware, certain software program, or electronic component may do business with banks, insurance companies, or accounting firms, among others.

The first step in the selling process is consulting with clients. Sales representatives ask the client to detail his or her current and future technological needs. Often, customers do not know a lot about computer or electronics technology, so the representative must explain and "translate" specialized computer terminology, as well as answer many questions. Reps advise customers which system, peripherals, or software will best meet their needs and fit within their price range. When the customer makes a final choice, representatives handle paperwork, including financing plans, service agreements, and payment. They assemble the order or arrange for delivery and installation if requested. In some cases, they ring up the order at a cash register. At larger stores, a cashier may handle this task.

To keep up with technological advances, sales representatives must attend training sessions or continuing education classes. Sales representatives who specialize must also keep up with changing needs of particular industries, such as insurance or banking.

Education and Training

Classes in speech and writing help you learn how to present a product to large groups of people. Computer science and electronics classes will give you a basic overview of the field. General business and math classes are also helpful.

Computer sales representatives who specialize in a specific industry, such as health care or banking, need training in current issues of that field. Such training is available through special work training seminars, adult education classes, or courses at a technical school. Many companies require their sales staff to complete a company training program where they learn the technologies and work tools they need.

Computer and electronics sales representatives need to know a little about a large number of products. They also need to know about the computer and

Tips for Success

To be a successful computer and electronics sales representative, you should

- have strong sales skills
- be a good listener
- be able to communicate with customers who have varying levels of technical knowledge
- be a "people person"
- be willing to pursue continuing education throughout your career

electronics industries as a whole so they can better advise their customers. Many manufacturers provide product introductions and hands-on training sessions specifically to help salespeople sell their products.

Earnings

Electronics and computer sales representatives working in retail start out earning an hourly wage—usually minimum wage. As of this writing, the federal minimum wage is $7.25 an hour (or $15,080 annually). In addition, they may earn commissions, or a percentage of sales they make. According to the U.S. Department of Labor, earnings of all retail sales representatives ranged from less than $25,000 to $104,000 or more in 2008.

Words to Learn

browser user-friendly software that makes Internet searches quicker and more efficient

hardware the physical components of a computer system; they typically include the motherboard, disk drives, display, keyboard, and the central processing unit

Internet a worldwide system of computer networks connected to each other

network two or more computers that are electronically connected to share data and programs

peripheral an auxiliary device (such as a modem, monitor, or disk drive) that is connected to a computer

software programs that tell the hardware what to do and how to do it

storage device device such as a CD-ROM, DVD-ROM, external hard drive, or flash drive that stores computer files outside of the computer

system in terms of computers, a group of computers and related technology that is linked together electronically

FOR MORE INFO

For information on careers, contact
Association for Computing Machinery
2 Penn Plaza, Suite 701
New York, NY 10121-0701
800-342-6626
acmhelp@acm.org
http://www.acm.org

For industry information, contact the
following organizations:
**Electronics Representatives Association
International**
300 West Adams Street, Suite 617
Chicago, IL 60606-5109

312-527-3050
info@era.org
http://www.era.org

North American Retail Dealers Association
222 South Riverside Plaza, Suite 2160
Chicago IL 60606-6160
800-621-0298
nardasvc@narda.com
http://www.narda.com

Outlook

Employment for computer and electronics sales representatives
should be excellent during the next decade. There will be career opportunities with computer specialty stores or consulting
companies that deal directly with businesses and their corporate computer and application needs.

Computer and Office Machine Service Technicians

What Computer and Office Machine Service Technicians Do

Computers and office machines are incredibly complex. It takes highly skilled electronics technicians to keep them working properly and efficiently. Computer and office machine service technicians service, install, calibrate, operate, maintain, and re-

EXPLORING

- Read books and magazines about computer and office machine repair. Here is one book suggestion: *Upgrading & Fixing PCs For Dummies*, 7th edition, by Andy Rathbone. Although it is geared toward high school students and adults, it will give you a general introduction to the field.
- Participate in school computer clubs.

- Try building your own computer or repairing discarded computer equipment.
- Talk to a service technician about his or her career. Ask the following questions: What type of tools and equipment do you use to do your job? What do you like most and least about your job? How did you train for the field? What advice would you give to someone who is interested in the career?

pair computers, peripherals (an auxiliary device such as a monitor or disk drive that is connected to a computer), and other office machines.

Computer and office machine service technicians work for computer manufacturers, large corporations, or repair shops. Technicians who work for manufacturers learn how their company's products work and how to repair them when they break. Sometimes, technicians are employed by computer manufacturers at a customer's workplace, where they help plan and install new computer systems. They also perform regular maintenance to make sure the equipment continues to operate properly. If the equipment breaks down, technicians fix it.

Some technicians work in the maintenance or service departments of large corporations. They work with many different types of machines, both mechanical and electronic.

Some computer and office machine service technicians work for companies or repair shops that specialize in providing maintenance services to computer and office machine users. When equipment breaks down or needs regular maintenance, technicians travel to the customers' offices to provide the necessary services.

Some very experienced computer and office machine service technicians own their own repair shops. To remain competitive and be successful, they may have to service a wide range of equipment or sell related products such as paper, ink, and toner for printers, fax machines, scanners, and photocopiers. In addition to technical skills, these entrepreneurs need knowledge of the basics of running a business, including bookkeeping and advertising.

Education and Training

Because computers and office machines are so complex, the technicians who work on them must have excellent electrical,

A technician repairs an office copy machine. (Bob Daemmrich, The Image Works)

mechanical, and engineering skills. Knowledge of computer programming is important in some work settings. Familiarity with the Internet and different types of software will come in handy. In addition, technicians must be able to follow written and spoken instructions and be able to communicate well. To develop these skills, take high school classes in computer science, mathematics, the physical sciences, shop, as well as English and speech classes.

The best way to prepare for this career is to attend a two-year technical training program after high school. These programs are offered by technical institutes and some community colleges. Large companies may offer on-the-job training to new hires. The training typically lasts several months and includes a week of classroom instruction, with the rest of the time spent working closely with an experienced technician at job sites.

Earnings

According to the U.S. Department of Labor, in 2008, computer and office machine service technicians earned average annual salaries of $37,810. Those just starting out in the field earned less than $23,000. Very experienced technicians earned $59,000 or more. Technicians with extensive work experience and certification earn more.

Words to Learn

bench servicer a repairer who works only in a shop area and does not make house calls

calibrate to adjust precisely according to specifications

computer peripherals any equipment linked to a computer hard drive such as disk drives, monitors, printers, and modems

diagnostic tests tests run on various mechanical and electronic machines to determine particular problems

field service representative a repairer who makes service calls at the client's business

troubleshoot to solve a problem step by step, checking first for the simplest causes and moving up to the more complex ones

Outlook

Employment opportunities for computer and office machine technicians are expected to be limited during the next decade. Computers and office machines are more reliable than in the past, and equipment that does malfunction is often replaced instead of fixed. Despite this prediction, there should continue to be demand for qualified and skilled technicians as government,

DID YOU KNOW?

- The history of office machines goes back to ancient Babylonia (modern-day Iraq) and the invention of the abacus, a manual calculating device. The abacus is considered an ancestor of the computer.
- In the 17th century, French mathematician and philosopher Blaise Pascal developed the first digital machine that could perform addition and subtraction. American inventor William Burroughs developed the first truly practical adding machine in 1894.
- The typewriter's history dates to the 19th century, although at this time many cumbersome typing machines were as big as pianos, and others resembled clocks. By the 1870s the Remington Company was producing much more practical machines. Thomas Edison invented the first electrically operated typewriter in 1872, and by the 1930s, such machines were being used in offices.
- The computer is the most recently engineered office machine. The first experimental versions of modern computers were built during the 1940s. Technical improvements made during the 1950s led to the first commercial computers. By the late 1950s and early 1960s, the transistor had been developed, and in the late 1960s integrated circuitry led to the development of minicomputers. In the early 1970s, the microprocessor became the heart of the modern computer. The development of the silicon chip, also known as the microchip, opened up many new uses for computers and related technology. Today, computers and related technologies are used in almost every business.

FOR MORE INFO

For information on careers, contact
Association for Computing Machinery
2 Penn Plaza, Suite 701
New York, NY 10121-0701
800-342-6626
acmhelp@acm.org
http://www.acm.org

For industry and certification information, contact the following organizations:
ACES International
5381 Chatham Lake Drive
Virginia Beach, VA 23464-5400
757-499-2850
aces@acesinternational.org
http://www.acesinternational.org

CompTIA
1815 South Meyers Road, Suite 300
Oakbrook Terrace, IL 60181-5228
630-678-8300
http://www.comptia.org

Electronics Technicians Association
5 Depot Street
Greencastle, IN 46135-8024
800-288-3824
eta@eta-i.org
http://www.eta-i.org

Institute for Certification of Computing Professionals
2350 East Devon Avenue, Suite 281
Des Plaines, IL 60018-4602
800-843-8227
office2@iccp.org
http://www.iccp.org

International Society of Certified Electronics Technicians
3608 Pershing Avenue
Fort Worth, TX 76107-4527
800-946-0201
info@iscet.org
http://www.iscet.org

hospitals, businesses (especially those conducting e-commerce), and universities continue to rely on computers to help manage their daily business. Technicians with experience, certification, and training in electronics will have the best job prospects.

Computer and Video Game Designers

What Computer and Video Game Designers Do

Computer and video game designers create the games played on computers and game consoles, in arcades, and on cell phones and the Internet. They think up new game ideas, including sound effects, characters, story lines, and graphics. Some de-

EXPLORING

- Read magazines like *Computer Graphics World* (http://www.cgw.com) and *Game Developer* (http://www.gdmag.com). They have articles about digital video and other technical and design information.
- Read books about computer and video game design. Here are a few suggestions: *Game Creation for Teens*, by Jason Darby; *Game Design for Teens*, by Les Pardew; and *Game Art for Teens*, 2d edition, by Les Pardew.

- Visit http://archives.igda.org/breakingin to read "Breaking In: Preparing for Your Career in Games."
- Write stories, puzzles, and games to work on your storytelling and problem-solving skills.
- Ask your teacher or counselor to help set up a presentation with a game designer.
- Try to design easy games, or experiment with games that have an editor.

signers, also known as *developers*, work full time for the companies that make the games. Or they might work part time as freelancers, making the games in their own studios, and then sell their ideas and programs to production companies.

Each game must have a story as well as graphics and sound that will entertain and challenge the players. A game begins with careful planning and preparation. Designers write scripts, sketch storyboards, decide how the characters and places should look, and make notes on sound effects and other features.

Designers use computer programs, or write their own programs to assemble text, art, and sound for the game. Reviewing the programs is a long trial-and-error process of correcting problems and smoothing rough spots. Designers usually create a basic game and then design several levels of difficulty for beginning to advanced players. It takes about six to 18 months to design a computer or video game.

Designing computer games often requires a whole team of workers, including programmers, artists, musicians, writers, and animators. Computer and video game designers have a unique combination of highly technical skills and vivid imaginations.

Computer and video game designers work in office settings, whether at a large company or a home studio. At some companies, artists and designers sometimes find themselves working

DID YOU KNOW?

- Sixty-eight percent of American households play video games.
- Forty percent of game players are women.
- Twenty-five percent of game players are under the age of 18.
- The most popular video game genres (by units sold) in 2008 were action (20 percent), family entertainment (19.3 percent), sports games (15.3 percent), shooter (10.9 percent), and racing (8.4 percent).
- The most popular computer game genres (by units sold) in 2008 were strategy (34.6 percent), role-playing (19.6 percent), family entertainment (17.1 percent), and shooter (9.7 percent).

Source: 2009 Essential Facts about the Computer and Video Game Industry, Entertainment Software Association

Tips for Success

To be a successful computer and video game designer, you should

- love playing computer and video games
- be creative and imaginative
- stay up to date with ever-changing computer technology
- have good communication skills in order to work well with programmers, writers, artists, musicians, electronics engineers, production workers, and others
- have good writing and design skills
- be able to work under deadline pressure
- be flexible about design and schedule changes

24 or 48 hours at a time, so the office areas are set up with sleeping couches and other areas where employees can relax. Because the game development industry is competitive, many designers find themselves under a lot of pressure from deadlines, design problems, and budget concerns.

Education and Training

If you want to be a computer and video game designer, you need to learn many different computer skills, including programming languages such as C++, Java, or Python. Take many computer classes in high school; some schools may even offer introductory courses on game design and animation. Art, literature, and music classes can help you develop your creativity.

You don't necessarily need a college degree to be a game designer, but most companies prefer to hire those with a bachelor's degree. Many schools now offer training programs that teach people how to design computer games. Recommended college courses include programming (including assembly level), computer architecture, software engineering, computer graphics, data structures, algorithms, game design, communication networks, artificial intelligence and expert systems, interface systems, mathematics, and physics.

FOR MORE INFO

For industry information, contact
Entertainment Software Association
575 7th Street, NW, Suite 300
Washington, DC 20004-1611
esa@theesa.com
http://www.theesa.com

For a list of colleges that offer game
design programs and plenty of career
information, including "Breaking In:

Preparing for Your Career in Games," visit
the association's Web site.
International Game Developers Association
19 Mantua Road
Mt. Royal, NJ 08061-1006
856-423-2990
contact@igda.org
http://www.igda.org

Earnings

Earnings depend on how much experience you have, where you live, the size of the company you work for, and whether you earn bonuses and royalties (a percentage of profits from each game that is sold). Game designers had average salaries of approximately $67,379 in 2008, according to *Game Developer* magazine. Game designers with less than three years of experience earned approximately $46,208. Those with three to six years' experience averaged $54,716 annually, and those with more than six years' experience averaged $74,688 per year.

Outlook

The computer and video game industry is growing quickly, with more and more companies hiring skilled people at many levels. Designers should find good job opportunities in the next 10 years as companies try to keep up with the demand for new games on a variety of new platforms, including the Internet.

Computer Network Specialists

What Computer Network Specialists Do

A computer network is a system of computer hardware, such as computers, terminals, printers, and other equipment, which is linked together electronically. Networks allow many users to share computer equipment and software at the same time. Networks also allow busy workers to share files, view one another's schedules, and otherwise share information.

EXPLORING

- Read books and magazines about computer networking.
- Join computer clubs at school and community centers.
- Ask your school district officials about the possibility of working with the school system's network specialists for a day or longer. Parents' or friends' employers might also be a good place to find this type of opportunity.
- Volunteer at local charities that use computer networks in their offices. Since many charities have small budgets, they may offer more opportunities to gain experience with some of the simpler networking tasks.
- Experiment by creating networks with your own computer, those of your friends, and printers, modems, fax machines, or other peripherals.
- Talk to a computer network specialist about his or her career.

Database management, which is the quick search and retrieval of needed information from a collection of data, is probably the most frequent use of computer networks in offices. Companies use database management in many ways. For example, a database for an inventory of parts and materials at a factory might include product names and numbers, date of purchase, and manufacturers' names. Other applications include management of airline reservations, medical records at hospitals, legal records for insurance companies, and files that specify the locations and capacities of water pipes maintained by a city's public works office.

Computer network specialists make sure computer networks run properly at all times. They install, maintain, update, and repair network equipment and files. They also help train people in how to use the network. Sometimes, they help a company decide which computer system to buy and help change existing software to better meet the needs of the business.

Network and computer systems administrators design, install, and manage computer networks. They work with the files and directories on the network's central computer, called the server. The server holds important files, including software applications and databases, all of which must be updated regularly. Some networks have separate servers for specific operations, such as communications or printing or databases. They also oversee local area networks (LAN), wide area networks (WAN), and Internet and intranet systems.

Network security specialists concentrate most of their efforts on making sure that the computer system is safe from illegal activity. Security is very important because most companies store private or confidential information on their computers. Network security specialists can tell when unauthorized changes are made in the files and who makes them. They report these problems and devise better ways to eliminate such errors in the future. For example, one important school database that must

A network administrator at an elementary school uses a laptop computer to check the functionality of a wireless network. (Al Goldis, AP Photo)

be protected by security specialists involves student grades; only authorized workers have access to these files.

   Data recovery operators set up emergency computer sites in case the main computers experience major problems. Business emergencies, for example, can be caused by natural disasters, such as power outages, floods, and earthquakes. Data recovery operators choose alternative locations, decide which hardware and software should be stored there, and decide how often files should be backed up (copied).

To be a successful computer network specialist, you should enjoy complex and detailed work. You should be well organized and patient. Network specialists enjoy challenges and problem solving. They are logical thinkers. You must also be able to communicate complex ideas in simple terms, and be able to work well under pressure and deadlines. As a network specialist, you should be naturally curious about the computing field. You must always be willing to learn more about new and different technologies.

DID YOU KNOW?

Where Computer Network Specialists Work

- Insurance companies
- Banks and other financial institutions
- Health care organizations
- Federal, state, and local government agencies
- Colleges and universities
- Nonprofit organizations
- Any company or organization that uses computer networks

Words to Learn

database a collection of information stored on a computer

debugging identifying and correcting errors in software

hardware the physical components of a computer system; they typically include the motherboard, disk drives, display, keyboard, and the central processing unit

LAN (Local Area Network) a network that exists at one location, typically an office

network two or more computers that are electronically connected to share data and programs

software programs that tell the hardware what to do and how to do it

WAN (Wide Area Network) a network that includes remote sites in different buildings, cities, states, or countries

wireless network a telecommunications network that uses electromagnetic waves, rather than wires, to transmit information

FOR MORE INFO

For information on careers, contact
Association for Computing Machinery
2 Penn Plaza, Suite 701
New York, NY 10121-0701
800-342-6626
acmhelp@acm.org
http://www.acm.org

For information on career opportunities
for women in computing, contact
Association for Women in Computing
41 Sutter Street, Suite 1006
San Francisco, CA 94104-4905
info@awc-hq.org
http://www.awc-hq.org

For information on careers, contact
IEEE Computer Society
1730 Massachusetts Avenue, NW
Washington, DC 20036-1992
202-371-0101
http://www.computer.org

For information on careers, contact
Network Professional Association
1401 Hermes Lane
San Diego, CA 92154-2721
888-NPA-NPA0
http://www.npa.org

For information on system
administration, contact the following
organizations:
**The League of Professional System
Administrators**
15000 Commerce Parkway, Suite C
Mount Laurel, NJ 08054-2212
http://www.lopsa.org

SAGE
c/o USENIX Association
2560 9th Street, Suite 215
Berkeley, CA 94710-2565
510-528-8649
office@sage.org
http://www.sage.org

Education and Training

Classes in math, science, and computers will help you prepare for this career. Business courses will help you understand how important business decisions, especially those relating to the purchase of expensive computer equipment, are made. English and speech classes will help you to develop your communication skills.

Computer network specialists typically have bachelor's degrees in computer science, information science, or management information systems. Some experienced workers may be hired with just an associate's degree and professional certification. More specialized positions require an advanced degree. Some people enter the field by first working as computer support specialists.

Earnings

Salaries for computer network specialists vary based on the size and type of employer, their level of experience, and specific job duties. The median yearly income for computer network and systems administrators was $66,310 in 2008, according to the U.S. Department of Labor. Salaries ranged from less than $41,000 to more than $104,000. Computer network specialists with experience and certification earn the highest salaries.

Outlook

Employment for computer network specialists is expected to be excellent during the next decade. Network specialists, particularly those with Internet and computer security experience, are in strong demand. The most jobs will be found in the computer systems design, software publishing, data processing and hosting, and technical consulting industries.

Computer Programmers

What Computer Programmers Do

Computer programmers write and code the instructions for computers. Programmers work for companies that create and sell computer hardware and software. They also work for all kinds of businesses, from manufacturers of office machines to distributors of machinery and equipment. They work for banks, hospitals, schools, and the federal government.

Programmers break down each step of a task into a series of instructions that the computer can understand. Then programmers translate the instructions into a specific computer language. (Java, C++, and Python are examples of computer languages.) Then programmers test the program to make sure it works. They correct any errors. This is called debugging the program. Finally, they write the instructions for the operators who will use the program. They also update, repair, and modify existing software programs. Programmers often work together on teams for a large project. In these situations, programmers may use computer-assisted software engineering tools, which automate much of the software coding. This allows them to focus on writing the unique parts of the program.

There are two basic kinds of computer programmers: *systems programmers* and *applications programmers.* Systems programmers must understand and care for an entire computer system, including its software, its memory, and all of its related equipment, such as terminals, printers, and disk drives. Systems programmers often help applications programmers with complicated tasks. Applications programmers write the programs that do

EXPLORING

- You will find countless books on programming at your local library or bookstore. There are plenty of resources to teach yourself no matter how much experience you have. Here are a few suggestions: *Hello World!: Computer Programming for Kids and Other Beginners*, by Warren and Carter Sande; *Visual Basic Game Programming for Teens*, by Jonathan S. Harbour; and *Game Programming for Teens*, 3rd edition, by Maneesh Sethi.
- The best way to learn about computers is to use one—either at home surfing the Internet or at school.
- Try to get some hands-on experience programming a computer.
- Join a computer club and find others who are interested in computers and programming.
- Talk to a computer programmer about his or her career.

particular tasks—word processing, accounting, databases, and games. They usually specialize in a field, such as business, engineering, or science.

One example of a programming specialty is numerical tool programming. *Numerical control tool programmers,* or *computer numerical control (CNC) programmers,* write programs that direct machine tools to perform their functions automatically. CNC programmers must understand how various machine tools operate and also know the properties of the metals and plastics that are used in the process. In direct numerical control, several machines are controlled by a central computer.

Another specialty is graphics programming. *Graphics programmers* write software programs that enable computers to produce designs, illustrations, and animations that help busi-

Alphabet Soup

- ASCII: American Standard Code for Information Interchange
- BPS: bits per second
- CPU: central processing unit
- DPI: dots per inch
- FTP: file transfer protocol
- GUI: graphical user interface
- HDD: hard disk drive
- HTTP: hypertext transmission protocol
- ISP: Internet service provider
- LAN: Local Area Network
- NQS: network queuing system
- RAM: random access memory
- ROM: read only memory
- URL: uniform resource locator
- WAN: Wide Area Network

ness, industry, and schools. Animations, designs, and illustrations may also be used for entertainment purposes, such as in video games or animated films.

As more programming functions become automated, programmers are increasingly taking on duties that were previously handled only by software engineers, such as designing certain parts of computer programs.

Education and Training

Take computer programming and computer science courses in high school. You should also focus on math courses. Other important classes include English and speech.

Most employers prefer to hire college graduates, although some talented students may be able to get a job with an associate's degree or certificate. Many colleges offer courses and degree programs in computer science, programming, mathematics, information systems, or related fields. Some employers may want their programmers to be trained in their specific area. For example, a computer programmer for an engineering firm might need an engineering degree. Other programmers may have degrees in accounting, finance, or business with a specialization in computer programming.

Words to Learn

alpha test the first test of newly developed hardware or software in a laboratory setting

beta test test of hardware or software performed by actual users under normal operating conditions

debug to search for and correct errors in a program

documentation written instructions explaining how to operate the program

flowchart a diagram that shows step-by-step progression through a procedure or system

hardware the physical components of a computer

log files plain text files used by programmers to track what the computer is doing while it is being used; they are typically used when a programmer is trying to look for errors in a program

software programs, procedures, and related documentation associated with a computer system

user interface the manner in which a user interacts with a computer, computer program, or computer system

Earnings

According to the National Association of Colleges and Employers, the average starting salary for college graduates with bachelor's degrees in computer science was $61,047 in July 2009. The average earnings for full-time programmers were about $69,620 a year in 2008, according the U.S. Department of Labor. Very experienced programmers earned more than $111,000 a year.

Outlook

Employment for computer programmers is expected to decline during the next decade. The increasing ability of people to write

FOR MORE INFO

For information on careers, contact
Association for Computing Machinery
2 Penn Plaza, Suite 701
New York, NY 10121-0701
800-342-6626
acmhelp@acm.org
http://www.acm.org

For information on career opportunities for women in computing, contact
Association for Women in Computing
41 Sutter Street, Suite 1006
San Francisco, CA 94104-4905
info@awc-hq.org
http://www.awc-hq.org

For industry information, contact
Association of Information Technology Professionals
401 North Michigan Avenue, Suite 2400
Chicago, IL 60611-4267
http://www.aitp.org

For information on computer careers and student programs, contact
IEEE Computer Society
1730 Massachusetts Avenue, NW
Washington, DC 20036-1992
202-371-0101
http://www.computer.org

For information on certification, contact
Institute for Certification of Computing Professionals
2350 East Devon Avenue, Suite 281
Des Plaines, IL 60018-4602
800-843-8227
office2@iccp.org
http://www.iccp.org

their own software programs and the transfer of programming jobs overseas have reduced demand for programmers. Despite this prediction, there should continue to be jobs for computer programmers. New workers will be needed to replace programmers who retire or leave the field for other jobs. The best opportunities will be available to those with college degrees, certification, and knowledge of new programming languages.

Computer Security Specialists

What Computer Security Specialists Do

Computer security specialists protect a company's computer network from intrusion by outsiders. These intruders are called *hackers*. The process of breaking into a system is called *hacking*. Computer security specialists are sometimes known as *Internet security specialists, Internet security administrators, Internet security engineers, information security technicians,* or *network security consultants* or *specialists.* A computer security specialist may work as a consultant (someone brought in from outside the company to work on a project) or as an employee (someone who works full time for that company).

When a company connects to the Internet, computer security specialists set up systems known as firewalls. Firewalls act as barriers of protection between the outside world of the Internet and the company by limiting or permitting access to data.

In-house computer security specialists are in charge of watching the flow of information through the firewall. They must be able to write computer code and set up, or configure, the software to alert them when certain kinds of activities occur. They monitor all access to the network and watch for anything out of the ordinary. If they see something strange, they investigate and sometimes track down the user who initiated the unusual action. Specialists may create a new program to prevent that action from happening again.

Computer security specialists are also in charge of virus protection. Viruses are computer programs written to pur-

EXPLORING

- National news magazines, newspapers, and trade magazines are great sources of information on current trends and hiring practices. Read professional publications such as *Information Security* (http://www.infosecuritymag.com). Another publication to consider is the quarterly magazine *2600* (http://www.2600.com). While *2600* is aimed at hackers, reading the articles will give you an understanding of how some systems are broken into and help you develop your ability to think of defenses.
- Check out programming books from the local library and learn how to write simple code.
- School science clubs and competitions offer opportunities to experiment with computer programming. They also encourage you to work with other students and get experience working in teams.
- Surf the Web and research the many security issues that face users today. Check the various information security Web sites and organizations that deal with Internet security. Use a search engine and the keywords "Internet AND Security" or "Network AND Security" or "Information AND Security."
- Talk to a computer security specialist about his or her career.

posely harm a hard drive. They can enter a network through e-mail attachments or infected disks. Specialists may create the security policies for the company and educate employees about those policies.

Computer security specialists who work as consultants design and set up solutions for a company's security problems. They must understand the needs of the company, determine if there are ways that hackers can get into the company's network, and find ways to correct them.

Education and Training

Take as many computer science and programming classes as possible to prepare for this career. Spend time in your school's computer lab, learn how computers work, and play with the latest technologies.

A growing number of two- and four-year colleges offer classes and degrees in computer security. Many colleges offer degrees in computer science, networking, and programming. These majors will also give you a good background for the field. Many employers require computer security specialists to have a bachelor's degree in computer science. Some people can land jobs with just experience and certification.

Earnings

The field of Internet security is a high-paying career. The low end of the pay scale is $40,000

Computer Security in the Movies

War Games (1983)
Matthew Broderick plays a teenage computer genius who cracks into a government defense system and nearly starts another world war.

Sneakers (1992)
A high-tech team of security experts, led by Robert Redford, steals a black box that contains super secret security information.

The Net (1995)
Sandra Bullock's identity is altered by criminals who are trying to obtain computer data from her that may implicate them in a crime.

Hackers (1995)
Fisher Stevens is a hacker with a criminal mind who tries to frame a group of computer whizzes for his crimes. The whiz kids then use their hacking skills to prove their innocence.

Takedown (2000)
This movie is based on the real story of the capture of computer hacker Kevin Mitnick, played by Skeet Ulrich in the film.

DID YOU KNOW?

Each year, the Computer Security Institute (CSI) surveys computer security specialists to determine the most common criminal attacks on computer systems. In 2009, the most common attacks were malware infection (64.3 percent of respondents reported that this had occurred at their company); laptop/mobile device theft (42.2 percent); insider abuse of Net access or e-mail (29.7 percent); denial of service (29.2 percent); financial fraud (19.5 percent); password sniffing (17.3 percent); and exploitation of the wireless network (7.6 percent).

Source: *2009 CSI Computer Crime and Security Survey,* Computer Security Institute

a year and is probably what you would make in an entry-level position at a small company. The majority of computer security specialists make between $50,000 and $90,000 a year. If you have a lot of experience, certification, and an excellent reputation in the industry, you can earn more than $120,000 a year.

Outlook

Employment for computer security specialists will be very good during the next decade. The number of companies with Web sites is growing very quickly. As these companies connect their private networks to the Internet, they will need to protect their private information. Currently, the demand for Internet security specialists is greater than the supply, and this trend is expected to continue.

FOR MORE INFO

A federally funded organization, the CERT Coordination Center, studies, monitors, and publishes security-related activity and research.
CERT Coordination Center
4500 Fifth Avenue
Pittsburgh, PA 15213-2612
412-268-7090
cert@cert.org
http://www.cert.org

This professional organization for information security professionals provides education and training for its members.
Computer Security Institute
600 Harrison Street
San Francisco, CA 94107-1387
http://www.gocsi.com

For information on certification, contact
(ISC)²
1964 Gallows Road, Suite 210
Vienna, VA 22182-3814
866-462-4777
https://www.isc2.org

Computer Support Specialists

What Computer Support Specialists Do

Have you ever had a problem with your family computer? If so, your parents may be able to fix it. But sometimes the problem is too serious for your parents to solve. In this instance, they might call a *computer support specialist.* These workers are specially trained to investigate and solve computer problems. They listen to customer complaints, discuss possible solutions, and write technical reports.

Computer support can be divided into three areas—user support, technical support, and microcomputer support. *User support specialists,* also known as *help desk specialists,* answer calls from users who have problems with their computers. They listen carefully as the user explains the problem and describes the commands entered directly prior to the problem occurring. They then try to work with the user to resolve the problem. If the problem is user error, the support specialist explains the mistake and

EXPLORING

- Start working and playing on computers as much as possible. Many computer professionals became computer hobbyists at a very young age.
- Surf the Internet, read computer magazines, and join school or community computer clubs.
- Look for special computer classes and demonstrations in your area.
- Learn as many software programs as you can. Also learn about networks, hardware, and peripheral equipment.
- Help your friends and family troubleshoot computer problems.
- Talk to a computer support specialist about his or her career.

A support specialist at Quicken Loans monitors internal computer use in order to assist company employees with their support needs. (Paul Sancya, AP Photo)

teaches the correct procedure. If the problem is in the hardware or software, the specialist isolates the problem and recommends a solution. The support specialist may have to consult supervisors or programmers. *Internal user support specialists* help users from their own company with online services. *External user support specialists* offer aid to a company's customers.

Technical support specialists solve problems with a computer's operating system, hardware, or software. They use resources, such as engineers or technical manuals, to get more information. They may modify or reinstall software programs or replace hardware parts. Technical support specialists who work in large corporations oversee the daily operations of the various computer systems in their company, determine if upgrades (improved versions of software or hardware) are needed, and work with other computer experts to modify commercial software to the company's specific needs. Technical support specialists who work for hardware and software manufacturers solve problems over the phone or Internet, or they may visit a client's site. They answer questions about installation, operation, and customizing.

Words to Learn

application software program that helps you do word processing, build databases, or create spreadsheets, among other possibilities

backup copies of computer files on disk stored in a place other than the main worksite, to be used in case of an emergency

crash when a computer freezes up and must be rebooted in order to operate; a "hard drive crash" means the computer can't be repaired

data dictionary information about data, including name, description, source of data item, and keywords for categorizing and searching for data items

glitch a "bug," or error in programming, that causes interruptions or problems in computer operations

hardware the physical components of a computer system; they typically include the motherboard, disk drives, display, keyboard, and the central processing unit

network two or more computers that are electronically connected to share data and programs

peripheral an auxiliary device (such as a modem, monitor, or disk drive) that is connected to a computer

user a person who uses a computer

High Marks for Computer Support

Each year, the Association of Support Professionals evaluates the Web sites that provide online computer support. Below are the top-rated support sites of 2009. Visit their Web sites to learn about top-quality computer support.

Open Division
EMC Corp.
http://www.emc.com

Hewlett Packard (consumer)
http://www.hp.com/#Support

Juniper Networks
http://www.juniper.net/customers/support

Mentor Graphics
http://supportnet.mentor.com

Novell
http://www.novell.com/services

Verizon
http://www.verizon.com

Small Company Division
Ariba
http://www.ariba.com

Articulate
http://www.articulate.com/support

Blackbaud
http://www.blackbaud.com/support/support.aspx

TriZetto
http://www.trizetto.com

Microcomputer support specialists are responsible for preparing computers for delivery to a client, including installing the operating system and desired software. After the unit is installed at the customer's location, the support specialists might help train users on appropriate procedures and answer any questions they have. They help diagnose problems or, if they can't solve the problem, they refer the individual to other support specialists.

Computer support specialists work for computer hardware and software companies. They also work for information systems departments of large corporations, government agencies, financial institutions, insurance companies, schools, telecommunications companies, and health care organizations.

To be a successful computer support specialist, you should like to solve problems and have patience to work with people who may not know a lot about computers. You should work well under stress, think logically, and have good communication skills. Since this field changes constantly, you should be willing to learn about new technologies as they are developed.

Education and Training

In high school, take technical courses, such as computer science or electronics, that will help you develop logical and analytical thinking skills. Courses in math and science are also valuable for this reason. Since computer support specialists have to deal with computer programmers on the one hand and computer users who may not know anything about computers on the other, you should take English and speech classes to improve your communication skills.

Computer support specialists must have at least an associate's degree to enter the field. Some companies require that their support specialists have a bachelor's degree in computer science, computer engineering, or information systems. Computer support specialists may also receive on-the-job training that typically lasts three months, but may last up to a year. Since technology changes so rapidly, it is very important for support specialists to keep up with advancements in the industry. Throughout their careers, support specialists must pursue continuing education. This training may be offered by their employers, colleges and universities, hardware and software vendors, and private training institutions. Certification is also recommended.

FOR MORE INFO

For more information about careers, contact
Association for Computing Machinery
2 Penn Plaza, Suite 701
New York, NY 10121-0701
800-342-6626
acmhelp@acm.org
http://www.acm.org

For salary surveys and other information, contact
Association of Support Professionals
122 Barnard Avenue
Watertown, MA 02472-3414
617-924-3944
http://www.asponline.com

For information on certification, contact
CompTIA
1815 South Meyers Road, Suite 300
Oakbrook Terrace, IL 60181-5228
630-678-8300
http://www.comptia.org

For information on certification and tips on career development, contact
Help Desk Institute
102 South Tejon, Suite 1200
Colorado Springs, CO 80903-2242
800-248-5667
support@thinkhdi.com
http://www.thinkhdi.com

For information on computer careers, contact
IEEE Computer Society
1730 Massachusetts Avenue, NW
Washington, DC 20036-1992
202-371-0101
http://www.computer.org

For industry information, contact
Technology Services Industry Association
17065 Camino San Bernardo, Suite 200
San Diego, CA 92127-5737
858-674-5491
info@thesspa.com
http://www.tsia.com

Earnings

Computer support jobs are plentiful in areas where clusters of computer companies are located, such as northern California's San Francisco Bay area and the Seattle, Washington, area. Median annual earnings for computer support specialists were $43,450 in 2008, according to the U.S. Department of Labor. Salaries ranged from less than $26,000 to $70,000 or more.

Support specialists with advanced education, more demanding job duties, and certification can earn higher salaries.

Outlook

Employment for computer support specialists will be good during the next decade. Each time a new computer product is released to the market or another system is installed, there will be problems, whether from user error or technical difficulty. Therefore, there will always be a need for computer support specialists to solve the problems. The U.S. Department of Labor reports that the best opportunities will be available in the following industries: computer systems design and related services; data processing, hosting and related services; software publishing; and management, scientific, and technical consulting. As health care organizations use more computer technology to improve patient care and efficiency, they will also provide many new jobs.

Computer support specialists with bachelor's degrees, work experience, certification, and good technical and communication skills will have the best job prospects.

Computer Systems Analysts

What Computer Systems Analysts Do

Computer systems analysts help banks, government offices, and businesses understand their computer systems. Most organizations use computers to store data. They need analysts who can design computer systems and programs for the specific needs of a business, or even for the needs of just one department in a business.

Computer systems analysts work with both the hardware and software parts of computer systems. Hardware includes the large items such as the computer itself, the monitor, and the keyboard. Software includes the computer programs, which are written and stored on disks, and the documentation (the manuals or guidebooks) that goes with the programs. Analysts design the best mix of hardware and software for the needs of the company that employs them.

A computer systems analyst for the personnel department of a large company, for example, would first talk to the department manager about which areas of the business could be helped by computer technology. If the company started a new policy of giving employees longer paid vacations at Christmas, the manager might want to know how this policy has affected company profits for the month of December. The analyst can show the manager what computer program to use, what data to enter, and how to read the charts or graphs that the computer produces. The work of the analyst allows the manager to review the raw data. In this case, the numbers show that company profits were the same as in the previous Decembers. The manager can then decide whether to continue the company policy.

Once analysts have the computer system set up and operating, they offer advice on equipment and programming

EXPLORING

- Visit the Association for Computing Machinery's career Web site, http://computingcareers. acm.org, for information on career paths, a list of suggested high school classes, profiles of computer science students, and answers to frequently asked questions.
- Read books about computers and careers in the field. Here are some suggestions: *Careers for Computer Buffs & Other Technological Types*, 3rd edition, by Marjorie Eberts; *The Complete Idiot's Guide to Computer Basics*, 5th edition, by Joe Kraynak; *Absolute Beginner's Guide to Computer Basics*, 5th edition, by Michael Miller; and *How Computers Work*, 9th edition, by Ron White and Timothy Edward Downs.

- Play strategy games, such as chess. Such games are a good way to use analytic thinking skills while having fun. Commercial games range in themes from war simulations to world historical development.
- Learn everything you can about computers. Work and play with them on a daily basis.
- Ask your teacher or counselor to help you set up an informational interview with a computer systems analyst.
- You might want to try hooking up a computer system at home or school, configuring terminals, printers, and modems. This activity requires a fair amount of knowledge and should be supervised by a parent.

DID YOU KNOW?

- Approximately 532,000 computer systems analysts are employed in the United States. About 24 percent work in the computer systems design and related services industry.
- About 6 percent of computer systems analysts are self-employed.
- Some computer systems analysts work more than 50 hours a week.

Source: U.S. Department of Labor

changes. Often, people in a department each have their own computer, but they must be able to connect with and use information from each other's computers. Analysts must then work with all the different computers in a department or a company so the computers can connect with each other. This system of connected computers is called a network.

Systems analysts who conduct detailed testing of the systems they set up are called *software quality assurance analysts.* If they find a problem, they figure out what caused it and fix the problem.

Systems programmer-analysts are specialists who design and update software that is used in computer systems. They are often asked to write new software that solves a particular problem that the company has encountered.

To be a successful computer systems analyst, you should like to solve problems and know a lot about computer hardware and software. You should be able to work well with many types of people, from managers to data entry clerks. You must be able to learn about new technology quickly. This field is constantly changing. Finally, you should have good time-management skills, be able to work as a member of a team, and be able to work under deadline pressure.

Education and Training

Take advanced high school classes in math, science, and computer science to prepare for this work. Since analysts do a lot of proposal writing, it is a good idea to take English classes, too. Speech classes will help prepare you for making formal presentations to management and clients.

To work as a computer systems analyst in a scientific or technical environment, you will need at least a bachelor's degree in computer science, applied mathematics, information science, engineering, or the physical sciences. Those who work for businesses usually have a degree in a business-related field such as management information systems. Analysts in highly technical areas (aeronautics, for example) usually have graduate degrees as well. Many employers are now seeking applicants with a master's degree in business administration with a concentration in information systems.

In addition to a college degree, job experience as a computer programmer is very helpful. Many businesses choose computer programmers already on staff and train them on the job to be systems analysts. Computer systems analysts with several years of experience are often promoted into managerial jobs.

Earnings

Starting salaries for computer systems analysts averaged about $45,000 a year in 2008, according to the U.S. Department of Labor. After several years of experience, analysts can earn $75,000 a year. Computer systems analysts with many years of experience and a master's degree can earn $118,000 a year or more. Salaries for analysts in government are somewhat lower than the average for private industry. Earnings also depend on years of experience and the type of business you work for.

Outlook

Employment for computer systems analysts will be excellent during the next decade.

DID YOU KNOW?

Where Computer Systems Analysts Work

- Banks
- Colleges and universities
- Credit bureaus
- Data processing service firms
- Government agencies
- Hardware and software companies
- Insurance companies
- Manufacturing companies
- Publishing companies

FOR MORE INFO

For information on careers, contact
Association for Computing Machinery
2 Penn Plaza, Suite 701
New York, NY 10121-0701
800-342-6626
acmhelp@acm.org
http://www.acm.org

For information on career opportunities
for women in computing, contact
Association for Women in Computing
41 Sutter Street, Suite 1006
San Francisco, CA 94104-4905
info@awc-hq.org
http://www.awc-hq.org

For information on publications, contact
**Association of Information Technology
Professionals**
401 North Michigan Avenue, Suite 2400

Chicago, IL 60611-4267
http://www.aitp.org

For information on computer careers and
student programs, contact
IEEE Computer Society
1730 Massachusetts Avenue, NW
Washington, DC 20036-1992
202-371-0101
http://www.computer.org

For information on certification,
contact
**Institute for Certification of Computing
Professionals**
2350 East Devon Avenue, Suite 281
Des Plaines, IL 60018-4602
800-843-8227
office2@iccp.org
http://www.iccp.org

Businesses are using more computers. As a result, they will rely more and more on systems analysts to make the right purchasing decisions and to keep systems running smoothly. There is also an increasing focus on computer security and integrating new technologies into company networks. This will create new job opportunities for computer systems analysts.

Computer Trainers

What Computer Trainers Do

Today's employees and students need to know how to send e-mail, how to use the Internet, and how to use word processing programs. However, many people become frustrated when faced with a blank computer screen and a thick instruction manual. Sometimes, too, the computers and programs are too complex to be explained fully and clearly by a manual or an online help section. *Computer trainers* teach people how to use computers, software, and other new technology. When a business installs new hardware and software, computer trainers work one-on-one with the employees or lead group training sessions. They may also teach people over the Internet. With technology changing every day, computer trainers are often called upon for support and instruction.

Computer trainers teach people how to use computer programs. For example, a company's accounting department may hire a computer

EXPLORING

- Visit your local library or bookstore and surf the Internet to keep up with the latest software and technology. The Internet has thousands of sites about computers and computer training.
- Teach yourself as many software programs as you can.
- Teach new computer programs to your parents, grandparents, or younger sisters and brothers.
- Talk to a computer trainer about his or her career. Ask the following questions: What made you want to enter this career? What are your main and secondary job duties? What do you like least and most about your job? How did you train for this field? What advice would you give a young person who is interested in the field?

A computer trainer assists a clerk (right) *during a new computer training class.* (Jim Cole, AP Photo)

trainer to teach its accounting clerks how to use a spreadsheet program. These programs are used to make graphs and charts, and to calculate sums. Other common business programs include database programs, which keep track of such things as customer names, addresses, and phone numbers, and word processing programs, which are used to create documents, letters, and reports. Some computer trainers may also teach computer programming languages such as C++, Java, or Python.

Many corporations, advertisers, and individuals have set up Web sites. A computer trainer can help them use the computer language needed to design a page, and teach them how to update the page. Trainers teach people how to operate desktop publishing programs and high-quality laser printers that allow individuals and businesses to create interesting graphics and full-color pages for brochures and newsletters. Some computer trainers may also help clients set up their own office network. With a network, all the computers in an office can be linked so that employees can share programs and files.

Computer trainers may be self-employed and work on a freelance basis, or they may work for a computer training school or computer service company.

To be a successful computer trainer, you should have excellent teaching skills and be excited about sharing knowledge with others. You should also have an outgoing personality since you will constantly be communicating with your students. Patience is also important because people learn at different rates, and you may have to repeat a lesson many times before a person understands. Since technology changes constantly, you will need to continue to learn throughout your career.

Education and Training

Take as many computer and mathematics classes as possible in high school. These will provide the foundation for the rest of your computer education. Speech, drama, or other performance courses will also help get you used to speaking in front of a crowd.

Most community colleges, universities, and vocational schools offer computer courses. Computer service companies and training schools also offer courses in specific software pro-

DID YOU KNOW?

- Data processing systems developed during World War II. The amount of information that had to be collected and organized for war efforts became so great that it was not possible for people to prepare it in time to make decisions. A quicker way had to be invented.
- After the war, the new computer technology was put to use in other government operations as well as in businesses. The first computer used by civilians was installed by the Bureau of the Census in 1951 to help gather data from the 1950 census. At this time, computers were large (as big as a room) and required a lot of power to operate. Three years later, the first computer was installed by a business firm. Today, computers are used extensively in government agencies, industrial firms, banks, insurance agencies, schools, publishing companies, scientific laboratories, and homes. It is hard to imagine what our society would be like without computers.

grams. Though college courses and training are important, it helps to have experience too. You can get experience by working with computers and the Internet regularly, either at home or in the workplace.

Education requirements vary at computer training schools and computer service companies. To work as a teacher in a high school or community college, a bachelor's degree is the minimum requirement.

Earnings

The average training specialist earns about $45,000. Senior training specialists average $60,000 a year. Training managers earn about $75,000. According to a 2008 salary survey conducted by *Microsoft Certified Professional Magazine,* the average salary of the responding Microsoft Certified Trainers was $88,675. These figures do not include yearly bonuses (additional pay), which may add several thousand dollars to a trainer's in-

Teaching Techniques

Here are some techniques trainers use to keep the attention of their students.

Case study The trainer presents hypothetical (imaginary) scenarios to practice problem-solving skills.

Demonstration The trainer shows how to perform a task in front of the learners.

Expert panel A group of experts shares their ideas with each other and the audience.

Games Contests and matches are used to improve technical performance and encourage teamwork.

Programmed instruction Trainees work through a series of steps that help them learn specific skills.

Role play Two or more individuals act out a situation that might happen in the real workplace to practice interpersonal skills.

Source: The American Society for Training and Development

FOR MORE INFO

For a list of academic programs and resources in the computer training field, contact
American Society for Training and Development
1640 King Street, Box 1443
Alexandria, VA 22313-1443
703-683-8100
http://www.astd.org

For more information on computer training, contact
ITrain, International Association of Information Technology Trainers
PMB 616
6030-M Marshalee Drive
Elkridge, MD 21075-5987
410-567-5366
http://itrain.org

come. In general, salaries for computer trainers increase with the level of education.

Outlook

The outlook for computer trainers is excellent because more people are using computers and related technology than ever before. According to the American Society for Training and Development, the short life cycles of technology products, combined with more challenging job duties, will increase the demand for computer trainers.

Database Specialists

What Database Specialists Do

A collection of information stored in a computer is called a database. *Database specialists* set up and maintain databases. They purchase computer equipment and create computer programs that collect, analyze, store, and send information. They

EXPLORING

- Read books and magazines about databases. Here is one book suggestion: *The Manga Guide to Databases*, by Mana Takahashi.
- Ask your counselor or computer teacher to arrange for a database specialist to speak to your class at school or to arrange for a field trip to a company to see database specialists at work.
- The Association for Computing Machinery has a Special Interest Group on Management of Data (SIGMOD). The Resources page

of SIGMOD's Web site (http://www.sigmod.org) provides an index of public domain database software that you may want to check out.

- Join a computer club. School computer clubs offer a good way to learn about computers and meet others interested in the field.
- Volunteer to work on databases at your school, religious institution, or local charity.
- Talk to a database specialist about his or her career.

may sometimes move information from old databases to new ones. They work for utility companies, stores, investment companies, insurance companies, publishing firms, telecommunications firms, schools, and for all branches of government.

Some database specialists figure out the type of computer system their company needs. They meet with top-level company officials to discuss these needs. Together they decide what type of hardware and software will be required to set up a certain type of database. Then a *database design analyst* writes a proposal, or plan, that states the company's needs, the type of equipment that will meet those needs, and how much the equipment will cost.

Database specialists set up the computer system that the company buys. *Database managers and administrators* decide how to organize and store the information in the database. They create a computer program or a series of programs and train employees to enter information into computers.

Computer programs sometimes crash, or work improperly. Database specialists make sure that a backup copy of the program and the database is available in case of a crash. Specialists also must protect the database from people or organizations who are not supposed to see it. Many databases are now connected to the Internet. A company's database contains important, and sometimes secret, information.

Tips for Success

To be a successful database specialist, you should

- be organized
- be a strong logical and analytical thinker
- be able to analyze large amounts of information quickly
- have strong communication skills
- be willing to pursue continuing education throughout your career

DID YOU KNOW?

- There are approximately 120,400 database specialists employed in the United States.
- Fourteen percent of database specialists work in computer systems design and related services.
- Seven percent of database specialists are self-employed.
- Fourteen percent of database specialists work more than 50 hours a week.

Source: U.S. Department of Labor

Very large companies may have many databases. Sometimes it is necessary for these databases to share information. Database managers see to it that these different databases can communicate with each other, even if they are located in different parts of the country.

Education and Training

If you are interested in becoming a database specialist, you should take as many computer courses as possible. In addition, you should study mathematics, accounting, science, English, and communications.

A bachelor's degree in computer science or business administration is required for entry-level database administrators. A master's degree in business administration with a concentration in information systems is required by some employers. Some employers require that potential hires are certified.

Earnings

Database specialists earned an average of $69,740 in 2008, according to the U.S. Department of Labor. Those just starting out in the field earned less than $40,000. Very experienced database specialists earned $112,000 or more. Earnings vary with the size, type, and location of the organization as well as a person's experience, education, and job responsibilities. Database administrators and consultants working for major computer companies usually earn the highest salaries.

FOR MORE INFO

For industry information, contact
American Society for Information Science and Technology
1320 Fenwick Lane, Suite 510
Silver Spring, MD 20910-3560
301-495-0900
asis@asis.org
http://www.asis.org

For industry information, contact
Association of Information Technology Professionals
401 North Michigan Avenue, Suite 2400
Chicago, IL 60611-4267
http://www.aitp.org

For information on certification, contact
DAMA International
19239 North Dale Mabry Highway, #132
Lutz, FL 33548-5067

813-448-7786
info@dama.org
http://www.dama.org

For information on computer careers and student programs, contact
IEEE Computer Society
1730 Massachusetts Avenue, NW
Washington, DC 20036-1992
202-371-0101
http://www.computer.org

For information on certification, contact
Institute for Certification of Computing Professionals
2350 East Devon Avenue, Suite 281
Des Plaines, IL 60018-4602
800-843-8227
office2@iccp.org
http://www.iccp.org

Outlook

Employment opportunities will be very good for database specialists over the next decade. The use of computers and database systems in almost all business settings creates great opportunities for well-qualified database personnel.

Graphics Programmers

What Graphics Programmers Do

To perform properly, a computer must be told what to do, how to do it, and when to do it. These sets of instructions are called computer programs. *Programmers* write software that allows the computer to perform many different tasks. *Graphics program-*

EXPLORING

- Read books about computer programming. Here are a few suggestions: *Hello World!: Computer Programming for Kids and Other Beginners,* by Warren and Carter Sande; *Visual Basic Game Programming for Teens,* by Jonathan S. Harbour; and *Game Programming for Teens,* 3rd edition, by Maneesh Sethi.
- Work on your school newspaper or yearbook to get experience with graphics and illustration programs.
- Join a computer club, especially one that has other members

interested in programming.
- Start learning programming languages, such as C++, Java, and Python.
- Talk to a graphics programmer about his or her career. Ask the following questions: What made you want to become a graphics programmer? What do you like most and least about your job? How did you train for the field? What advice would you give to someone interested in the career? What is the employment outlook?

mers write software programs that enable the computer to produce designs, illustrations, and animations that are used for education, business and medical applications, and entertainment. Programmers use special computer languages, such as C++, Java, and Python, to write their programs.

Graphics programmers write the code that produces two- and three-dimensional illustrations with color, lighting, shading, morphing, and special effects, as well as computer animation. They create new programs for medical imaging devices; geological research; virtual testing systems for aircrafts, cars, and spacecraft; animation and graphics for computer and video games; and special effects and animation for Hollywood productions.

Graphics programmers are experts in math, particularly geometry and algorithms. (An algorithm is a step-by-step procedure for solving a problem.) They first look at what the final graphics should look like. For example, a medical school might want a computer program that shows various views of different parts of the human body. The program might show the skeletal system, muscles, organs, and vascular system. Each part of the body might need to be viewed from the front, side, and back, as well as in cross-section.

Graphics programmers create a flowchart to show the order in which a computer will process information to produce each view of each body part. They write code in a computer language

Tips for Success

To be a successful graphics programmer, you should

- be good at math
- be patient
- have good reasoning skills
- have strong writing and speaking skills
- be able to get along with all types of people who have varying levels of computer skills
- be willing to continue to learn throughout your career

DID YOU KNOW?

Where Graphics Programmers Work

- Software developers
- Educational publishers
- Government agencies
- Self-employed (consultants)
- Any companies or organizations that use computer graphics

that tells the computer mathematically how to draw the graphics. Programmers may use computer-assisted software engineering tools, which automate much of the software coding. This allows them to focus on writing the unique parts of the graphics. Once the initial program is completed, it goes through testing. Graphics programmers may have to rewrite code and debug (search for and correct errors) the program until it is ready to be used.

One major specialty in the field is graphics programming for computer and video games. These workers design software and write code in order to create the exciting action and elaborate virtual worlds of computer and video games. Another fast growing area is graphics programming for animated television shows and movies.

Education and Training

To become a graphics programmer, you must earn a college degree in computer science, computer programming, or a related field. To prepare for college, take courses in computer science, English, mathematics, science, and foreign languages. Art or graphic design courses will help you develop a good sense of composition, proportion, perspective, and other elements of visual art.

In college you should complete a general computer science program. Courses should include computer graphics but not be limited to graphics. There is much competition for computer programming jobs, so you might want to consider earning a graduate degree.

Earnings

According to the National Association of Colleges and Employers, starting salary offers in computer science averaged $61,407

FOR MORE INFO

For more information on computer graphics, contact
Association for Computing Machinery
Special Interest Group on Computer
    Graphics
2 Penn Plaza, Suite 701
New York, NY 10121-0701
800-342-6626
acmhelp@acm.org
http://www.acm.org

For information on computer careers, contact
IEEE Computer Society
1730 Massachusetts Avenue, NW
Washington, DC 20036-1992
202-371-0101
http://www.computer.org

in July 2009. The U.S. Department of Labor reports that median annual earnings of computer programmers were $69,620 in 2008. Programmers just starting out in the field earned less than $40,000 annually. Very experienced programmers with experience and advanced education earned more than $111,000. Computer programmers who worked for software publishers earned mean annual salaries of $81,780.

Outlook

Employment for computer programmers is expected to decline during the next decade. Technological advances have made it easier to write basic code, eliminating some of the need for programmers to do this work. More complex software has allowed more and more end users to design, write, and implement more of their own programs.

However, the specialty of graphics programming still has a promising future. As more applications for computer graphics are explored and businesses find ways to use graphics in their everyday operations, graphics programmers will be in demand.

Hardware Engineers

What Hardware Engineers Do

Computer *hardware engineers* work with the insides of a computer, including motherboards, memory chips, central processing units (CPUs), hard drives, CD-ROM drives, removable storage, video cards, sound cards, network cards, and modems. They improve, repair, and change parts to keep up with the demand for faster and stronger computers and better software programs.

Some hardware engineers specialize in the design of computers or microprocessors. Others specialize in designing and organizing information systems for business and the government. They may also work with peripheral devices, such as printers, scanners, keyboards, speakers, and monitors.

The first step for most hardware projects is to describe the new device and its function. Will it be a tiny electronic component such as a transistor? Will it be part of a huge industrial robot? Or will it be a microprocessor or other specialized board? Once they define the function, engineers design the actual component and make plans to build it.

Engineers need to consider the device's overall effectiveness and reliability, its cost, and safety. Once the device is made, it is tested and evaluated, several times if necessary. Sometimes engineers also design the machinery that will manufacture the device.

Tools such as computer-aided design help engineers create three-dimensional designs that are easily edited by a computer.

EXPLORING

- Read books and magazines about computers, especially those that focus on computer hardware. Here are some book suggestions: *The Complete Idiot's Guide to Computer Basics,* 5th edition, by Joe Kraynak; *Absolute Beginner's Guide to Computer Basics,* 5th edition, by Michael Miller; and *How Computers Work,* 9th edition, by Ron White and Timothy Edward Downs.

- Visit the Association for Computing Machinery's career Web site, http://computingcareers.acm.org, to learn more about computer engineering. Another recommended site is Why Choose Computer Science & Engineering? (http://www.cs.washington.edu/WhyCSE).

- Ask your computer teacher or counselor to set up an informational interview or job shadowing experience with a hardware engineer. You can also talk to your high school computer science teacher about the career.

- Join a computer club with others who are interested in hardware. You may find a mentor who can teach you about hardware components.

- Find someone who would be willing to give you old computers that they are going to throw away. Use the parts to reconstruct a new computer or fix one that needs repair. Examine various parts and see if you can tell how they are made.

Hardware engineers also use different network systems such as Local Area Networks (LAN) and Wide Area Networks (WAN), among others, as well as specific programming languages suited to their companies' needs. Many engineers work as part of a team of specialists who use science, math, and electronics to improve existing technology.

Education and Training

You can get a head start on your computer career by taking computer, electronics, and programming classes now. Being

Words to Learn

chip a small slice of a semiconductor material, such as silicon, that contains an integrated circuit

CPU (central processing unit) the part of a computer that carries out the instructions of a program

disk drive an electromechanical device that records data on, or obtains data from, a disk; also known as a hard drive

hardware the physical components of a computer

integrated circuit an interconnected array of tiny electronic components made on a single small piece of silicon or other semiconducting material

microprocessor a CPU on a single microelectronic chip

motherboard the main printed circuit board in a microcomputer; it contains various integrated circuits (including the microprocessor and RAM chips) and slots for expansion cards

network two or more computers that are electronically connected to share data and programs

peripheral an auxiliary device (such as a modem, monitor, or disk drive) that is connected to a computer

semiconductor the basic component of microchips; a solid, crystalline substance (especially silicon in electronics) with conducting properties between true conductors and insulators

software programs, procedures, and related documentation associated with a computer system

storage device device such as a CD-ROM, DVD-ROM, external hard drive, or flash drive that stores computer files outside the computer

transistor a small electronic device used in a circuit as a switch, detector, or an amplifier

able to communicate effectively with co-workers and clients is important, so prepare yourself by taking speech and writing courses.

Most computer professionals have a bachelor's degree in computer science or engineering. Many employers, though, prefer to hire people with a bachelor's or advanced degree in computer science.

Earnings

Starting salary offers in July 2009 for bachelor's degree candidates in computer engineering averaged $61,738, according to the National Association of Colleges and Employers. The U.S. Department of Labor reports that median annual earnings of computer hardware engineers were $97,400 in 2008. Salaries ranged from less than $59,000 to more than $148,000. Hardware engineers who worked in computer systems design and related services earned mean annual salaries of $98,160. Those who worked for the federal government earned $94,680.

> ## DID YOU KNOW?
>
> - Early forerunners of the computer were the abacus, developed in ancient times in the Far East, and an adding machine invented in 1641 by Blaise Pascal of France. The principle of using a punched card to encode information was developed in about 1801 by Joseph-Marie Jacquard, also of France. His cards were used to control the pattern produced in textiles by a loom (a device that is used to weave cloth).
> - All of the basic parts of the modern digital computer—input and output devices, storage and arithmetic units, and the sequencing of instructions—were conceived in the 1820s and 1830s by Charles Babbage, an English mathematician. He completed a small computer, called a "difference engine," in 1822. It consisted primarily of gears and levers and was similar to a mechanical desk calculator.

Outlook

Employment opportunities for hardware engineers will only be fair in the next decade. Many American companies are hiring foreign companies to meet their hardware engineering needs. These companies typically pay lower salaries than American companies. This will result in fewer opportuni-

FOR MORE INFO

To find out more about a career as a hardware engineer, contact

Association for Computing Machinery
2 Penn Plaza, Suite 701
New York, NY 10121-0701
800-342-6626
acmhelp@acm.org
http://www.acm.org

For information on career opportunities for women in computing, contact

Association for Women in Computing
41 Sutter Street, Suite 1006
San Francisco, CA 94104-4905
info@awc-hq.org
http://www.awc-hq.org

For certification information, contact

Institute for Certification of Computing Professionals
2350 East Devon Avenue, Suite 281
Des Plaines, IL 60018-4602
800-843-8227
office2@iccp.org
http://www.iccp.org

For information on computer careers and student programs, contact

IEEE Computer Society
1730 Massachusetts Avenue, NW
Washington, DC 20036-1992
202-371-0101
http://www.computer.org

ties for hardware engineers in the United States. One area of growth in the U.S. is computer systems design and related services. Hardware engineers with advanced degrees and experience will have the best job prospects.

Internet Transaction Specialists

What Internet Transaction Specialists Do

Internet transaction specialists design, develop, and set up Internet transaction software or systems. This software or system is the technology that allows a customer to buy a book or song online, for example, by giving his or her credit card number.

Every business engaged in e-commerce must use some type of Internet transaction software, which allows customers to purchase products and services, transfer money between banks, pay bills online, and buy and sell stocks. This process is also

EXPLORING

- Try to get hands-on experience working with computers.
- Read books about the Internet and computer security and experiment with Web development tools.
- Join your school's computer club.
- Keep up with the latest news by reading computer magazines and journals.

- Talk to an Internet transaction specialist about his or her career. Ask the following questions: What made you want to enter the field? What do you like most and least about your job? How did you train for your career? What advice would you give to someone interested in the career? How will the field change in the future?

DID YOU KNOW?

Where Internet Transaction Specialists Work

- Financial institutions
- Software developers
- Colleges and universities
- Any company that uses electronic funds transfer technology
- Self-employed (consultant)

referred to as electronic funds transfer. Transaction software and systems also allow businesses to get credit card approval for a customer's purchase, receive payments, and make money transfers. As e-commerce has become more and more popular, the need for Internet transaction specialists has grown.

One of the major responsibilities of a transaction specialist is to make sure that the system is secure. Because these transactions involve money and because they take place over the Internet, the possibility exists for cybercrime (crime that involves the use of the Internet, a computer, or other digital technology). Customers need to feel sure that their credit card numbers won't be stolen or their bank accounts emptied by hackers breaking into the system. (Hackers are people who use computers to illegally obtain financial, classified, or other confidential information.) Transaction specialists constantly work to improve systems, or protocols, for secure financial transactions.

Another major responsibility of the specialist is to improve software and systems so that transactions are faster and less complicated. This allows banks, credit card companies, and stores to exchange financial data more rapidly and directly.

On a daily basis, transaction specialists oversee the mechanical applications of the software and Web site. They provide technical support and solve customer service issues. Internet transaction specialists meet with managers to discuss changes or additions to services the company wants to offer its customers. Then they determine what type of programming is needed. Transaction specialists may work with other programmers to build the software and system.

Some companies have large enough e-commerce needs that they have their own in-house transaction specialists. Smaller companies may hire a firm specializing in e-commerce systems to perform this service. A transaction specialist who works for one of these firms may work on projects for a variety of clients.

To be an Internet transaction specialist, you should enjoy learning about new technology and be able to learn on your own as well as through organized classes. People in this field constantly improve their skills by reading about the latest developments and teaching themselves new techniques. You'll need the desire and initiative to keep up on new technology, software, and hardware. You must also have good verbal and written communication skills because you will often have to interact with a team or with the end user. Finally, you must be able to handle tight deadline pressures.

DID YOU KNOW?

The Internet developed from ARPANET, an experimental computer network established in the 1960s by the U.S. Department of Defense. By the late 1980s the Internet was being used by many government and educational institutions. In the early 1990s, public use of the Internet increased dramatically, spurred by the development of the Web.

The Web had its beginnings in 1991, when hypertext code was developed, primarily as a means of creating links between scholarly articles on the Internet. In 1993 the first Web browser, Mosaic, became available, developed by programmers at the University of Illinois. Mosaic added graphic capabilities to the existing system of links. Businesses quickly realized the commercial potential of the Web and soon developed their own Web sites. By October 2008, the number of sites on the Internet had grown to more than 182 million, according to Netcraft.

Education and Training

To prepare for a career as a transaction specialist, obtain as much computer training as you can get. Develop your analytical and problem-solving skills by taking mathematics classes such as algebra, geometry, and calculus. English classes will help you develop your communication, research, and writing skills.

Most companies require transaction specialists to have college degrees, preferably in computer science, computer engineering, mathematics, or business. Classes in information security will be useful since you will have to learn how to protect customers' private information from hackers. Work experience in programming gained through an internship or co-op program is beneficial.

Earnings

Salaries for Internet transaction specialists vary. They depend on factors such as experience, technical knowledge, geographic location, and the size of the employer. Salaries for junior programmers without much experience usually begin around $45,000 annually. On the other end of the scale, experienced professionals can earn as much as $200,000, though salaries between $75,000 and $100,000 are more common.

Outlook

Some of the fastest-growing careers in the next decade will be computer related. The future of transaction specialists will be closely tied to the future of e-commerce itself. If e-commerce continues to grow, then there will be good opportunities for transaction specialists. If business slows, there will be fewer opportunities. Job security with any one company may be uncertain. Mergers, business failures, downsizing, and ever-changing technology may cause some instability regarding

FOR MORE INFO

For industry information, contact
American Society for Information Science and Technology
1320 Fenwick Lane, Suite 510
Silver Spring, MD 20910-3560
301-495-0900
asis@asis.org
http://www.asis.org

For information on careers, contact
Association for Computing Machinery
2 Penn Plaza, Suite 701
New York, NY 10121-0701
800-342-6626
acmhelp@acm.org
http://www.acm.org

For information on career opportunities for women in computing, contact
Association for Women in Computing
41 Sutter Street, Suite 1006
San Francisco, CA 94104-4905
info@awc-hq.org
http://www.awc-hq.org

This center studies Internet security problems and provides security alerts. For industry news, visit its Web site.
CERT Coordination Center
Software Engineering Institute
Carnegie Mellon University
Pittsburgh, PA 15213-2612
412-268-7090
http://www.cert.org

For information on computer security, contact
Computer Security Institute
600 Harrison Street
San Francisco, CA 94107-1387
415-905-2626
http://gocsi.com

For information on computer careers and student programs, contact
IEEE Computer Society
1730 Massachusetts Avenue, NW
Washington, DC 20036-1992
202-371-0101
http://www.computer.org

long-term employment with any one firm. Specialists who stay current with technology and are willing to learn and adapt will be in high demand.

Microelectronics Technicians

What Microelectronics Technicians Do

Microelectronics technicians work in research laboratories to develop and construct custom-designed microchips. Microchips, often called simply "chips," are tiny but extremely complex electronic devices that control the operations of many kinds of communications equipment, consumer products (such as flat-screen televisions and MP3 players), industrial controls,

EXPLORING

- Read books and visit Web sites about microelectronics and computer technology.
- Join science, computer, or electronics clubs.
- Work on electronics projects at home. You can find many resources for electronics experiments and projects in your school or local library or on the Internet.
- Try to get a part-time job repairing electronic equipment. This will give you exposure to

the basics of electronics.

- Talk to a microelectronics technician about his or her career. Ask the following questions: What are your main and secondary job duties? What types of tools and equipment do you use to do your job? What do you like least and most about your career? How did you train for this field? What advice would you give a young person who is interested in the field?

DID YOU KNOW?

Where Microchips Are Used

- Calculators
- Computer and video games
- Computers
- DVD players
- Microwave technology
- MP3 players
- Radar
- Radio
- Robotics
- Space technology
- Television
- Weapons systems
- X-rays

aerospace guidance systems, and medical electronics. The process of manufacturing chips is called fabrication.

Microelectronics technicians usually work from a schematic prepared by an engineer. The schematic contains a list of the parts needed to construct the component and the layout that the technician will follow. The technician gathers the parts and prepares the materials to be used. Following the schematic, the technician constructs the component and then uses a variety of complex equipment to test the component's performance.

If the component doesn't work, microelectronics technicians troubleshoot the design, trying to find where the component has failed, and replace one part for a new or different part. Test results are reported to the engineering staff, and the technician may help evaluate the results and prepare reports.

After the testing period, the microelectronics technician often assists in the technical writing of the component's specifications. These specifications are used for integrating the component into new or redesigned products or for developing a process for the component's large-scale manufacture.

A technician studies an electronic component to ensure that it meets quality standards. (Bob Daemmrich, The Image Works)

Some microelectronics technicians specialize in the fabrication and testing of semiconductors and integrated circuits. These technicians are usually called *semiconductor development technicians.*

To be a successful microelectronics technician you should have a strong background in science and mathematics. You should also be able to work as a member of a team and have good communication skills. Other important traits for microelectronics technicians include attention to detail, patience, and the ability to follow instructions.

Education and Training

Classes in algebra, geometry, chemistry, and physics will prepare you for a postsecondary educational program or apprenticeship. Industrial classes, such as metalworking, wood shop,

Words to Learn

capacitor an element in an electrical circuit used to store a charge temporarily

conductor a substance that conducts an electrical charge

insulator a material that does not conduct electricity

integrated circuit a tiny chip of material imprinted or etched with many interconnected electronic components

microchip (or chip) a tiny slice of semiconducting material processed to hold specific electrical properties in order to be developed into an integrated circuit; also refers to an integrated circuit

resistor a device that provides resistance, used to control electric current

schematic a diagram that provides structural and/or procedural information on the construction of an electrical or mechanical system

semiconductor the basic component of microchips; a solid, crystalline substance (especially silicon in electronics) with conducting properties between true conductors and insulators

transistor a small, electronic device used in a circuit as a switch, detector, or an amplifier

FOR MORE INFO

For information on careers, contact
Association for Computing Machinery
2 Penn Plaza, Suite 701
New York, NY 10121-0701
800-342-6626
acmhelp@acm.org
http://www.acm.org

For information on computer careers and
student programs, contact
IEEE Computer Society
1730 Massachusetts Avenue, NW
Washington, DC 20036-1992
202-371-0101
http://www.computer.org

For information on certification, contact
**International Society of Certified
Electronics Technicians**
3608 Pershing Avenue
Fort Worth, TX 76107-4527
800-946-0201
info@iscet.org
http://www.iscet.org

For information on semiconductors,
a glossary of terms, and industry
information, contact
Semiconductor Industry Association
181 Metro Drive, Suite 450
San Jose, CA 95110-1344
408-436-6600
mailbox@sia-online.org
http://www.sia-online.org

auto shop, and machine shop, and similar courses in plastics, electronics, and construction techniques are helpful.

College education or training is a requirement for entering the field. Two-year training programs in electronics, highly automated systems, or electromechanical automation are offered at community colleges or vocational training facilities where you can earn a certificate or an associate's degree. There are also three- and four-year apprenticeship programs that include on-the-job training with an employer.

Earnings

According to the U.S. Department of Labor, median annual earnings of electrical and electronics engineering technicians (a job category that includes microelectronics technicians) were $53,240 in 2008. Salaries ranged from less than $32,000 to more than $78,000. Technicians who work as managers or supervisors earn higher salaries, ranging between $45,000 and $90,000 per year.

Outlook

Employment in the computer and electronic product manufacturing industry is expected to decline during the next decade, according to the U.S. Department of Labor. New electronic technology is lasting longer, which will reduce the number of technicians needed. Additionally, the use of advanced technologies, such as computer-aided design and drafting and computer simulation, will limit job growth.

Software Designers

What Software Designers Do

Without software, computers would not be able to work. The term *software* was coined to differentiate it from *hardware*, which refers to the physical parts of the computer system. Software is the set of mathematical codes that tells a computer what to do. A set of instructions that directs a computer's hardware to perform a task is called a software program. There are three types of software. *System software* controls a computer's internal functioning, usually through an operating system, and runs such extras as monitors, printers, and storage devices. *Application software* directs the computer to carry out commands given by the user. Application software includes word processing, spreadsheet, database management, inventory, and payroll programs. *Network software* coordinates communication between the computers that are linked in a network.

Software designers create software programs, also called applications. *Computer programmers* then create the software by writing the code that gives the computer instructions.

Software designers must imagine every detail of what a software application will do, how it will do it, and how it will look on the screen. An example is how a home accounting program is created. The software designer first decides what the program should be able to do, such as balance a checkbook, keep track of incoming and outgoing bills, and keep records of expenses. For each of these tasks, the software designer decides what menus and icons to use, what each screen will look like, and whether

EXPLORING

- Read books about computers and careers in the field. Here are some suggestions: *Careers for Computer Buffs & Other Technological Types*, 3rd edition, by Marjorie Eberts; *The Complete Idiot's Guide to Computer Basics*, 5th edition, by Joe Kraynak; *Absolute Beginner's Guide to Computer Basics*, 5th edition, by Michael Miller; and *How Computers Work*, 9th edition, by Ron White and Timothy Edward Downs.

- Visit the Association for Computing Machinery's career Web site, http://computingcareers. acm.org, for information on career paths, a list of suggested high school classes, profiles of computer science students, and answers to frequently asked questions about the field.

- Learn as much as you can about computers. Take computer classes in school, especially those that focus on software design and computer programming.

- Keep up with new technology by reading computer magazines, visiting computer Web sites, and by talking to other computer users.

- Join computer clubs.

- Advanced students can put their design and programming knowledge to work by designing and programming their own applications, such as simple games and utility programs.

- Talk to a software designer about his or her career.

there will be help or dialog boxes to assist the user. For example, the designer may want the expense record part of the program to produce a pie chart that shows the percentage of each household expense in the overall household budget. The designer can ask that the program automatically display the pie chart each time a budget is completed or only after the user clicks on a special icon on the toolbar.

Tips for Success

To be a successful software designer, you should

- be detail-oriented and patient
- enjoy problem-solving
- be able to work under deadline pressure
- have good communication skills
- be creative
- have excellent technical skills

Some software companies custom design software for the specific needs of one business. Some businesses are large enough that they employ in-house software designers who create software applications for their computer systems.

Software designers work throughout the United States, but opportunities are best in large cities and suburbs where business and industry are active. Programmers who develop software systems work for software manufacturers, many of which are in California's Silicon Valley. Software manufacturers are also clustered in Boston, Chicago, and Atlanta, among other places. Designers who adapt and tailor the software to meet specific needs of end-users work for those end-user companies, which are scattered across the country.

Education and Training

Computer, science, and math classes will prepare you for a career as a software designer. In high school you should take as many of these courses as possible. English and speech classes will help you improve your communication skills, which are important when making formal presentations to managers and clients once you enter the field.

To be a software designer, you will need at least a bachelor's degree in computer science plus at least one year of experience with a programming language. You also need knowledge of the field that you will be designing software for, such as education, entertainment, business, or science. For example, someone with a bachelor's degree in computer science with a minor in busi-

Helping Hands: Bill and Melinda Gates

Bill Gates is the founder (along with Paul Allen) of the computer giant Microsoft. He is the richest person in the world. With all of the money he ever could need, Gates could have retired from Microsoft and lived a life of luxury. Instead, he wanted to make a difference in the world. In 1994, he created the William H. Gates Foundation, which focused on improving world health. In 1997, he and his wife Melinda (a computer professional whom he met at Microsoft) created the Gates Library Foundation, which sought to bring computers with Internet connections to public libraries in the United States. This organization eventually refocused its mission to help low-income minority students prepare and pay for college. In 2000, the two organizations were merged to form the Bill & Melinda Gates Foundation. The foundation has awarded more than $21 billion in grants to organizations in the United States and more than 100 other countries. Bill and Melinda Gates travel the world advocating to end world poverty and support other causes. Visit http://www.gatesfoundation.org for more information about the foundation and Bill and Melinda Gates.

Source: Bill & Melinda Gates Foundation

ness or accounting has an excellent chance to land a job creating business and accounting software.

Earnings

Median salaries for computer and information scientists (a job category that includes software designers) were $97,970 in 2008, according to the U.S. Department of Labor. Software designers just starting out in the field earned less than $57,000. Very experienced workers earned more than $151,000. At the managerial level, salaries are even higher and can reach $175,000 or more.

FOR MORE INFO

For information on careers, contact
Association for Computing Machinery
2 Penn Plaza, Suite 701
New York, NY 10121-0701
800-342-6626
acmhelp@acm.org
http://www.acm.org

For information on career opportunities
for women in computing, contact
Association for Women in Computing
41 Sutter Street, Suite 1006
San Francisco, CA 94104-4905
info@awc-hq.org
http://www.awc-hq.org

For information on computer careers and
student programs, contact
IEEE Computer Society
1730 Massachusetts Avenue, NW

Washington, DC 20036-1992
202-371-0101
http://www.computer.org

For information on certification, contact
**Institute for Certification of Computing
Professionals**
2350 East Devon Avenue, Suite 281
Des Plaines, IL 60018-4602
800-843-8227
office2@iccp.org
http://www.iccp.org

For industry information, contact
**Software & Information Industry
Association**
1090 Vermont Avenue, NW, Sixth Floor
Washington, DC 20005-4095
202-289-7442
http://www.siia.net

Outlook

There will continue to be strong employment opportunities for software designers. Employment of software designers is expected to increase as technology advances. The expanding use of the Internet by businesses, as well as the growing use of software in cell phones and video games, has created great demand for skilled professionals to design software.

Software Engineers

What Software Engineers Do

Computers need to be told exactly what to do in order to function. Software is the set of mathematical codes that tells a computer what to do. A set of instructions that directs a computer's hardware to perform a task is called a program, or software program.

Businesses use computers to do complicated work for them. In many cases, their needs are so specialized that commercial software programs cannot perform the desired tasks. *Software engineers* change existing software or create new software to solve problems in many fields, including business, medicine, law, communications, aerospace, and science.

Software engineers fall into two basic categories. *Systems software engineers* build and maintain entire computer systems and networks for a company. *Applications software engineers* design, create, and modify general computer applications software or specialized utility programs.

The projects software engineers work on are all different, but their methods for solving a problem are similar. First, engineers talk to clients to find out their needs and to determine the problems they are having. Next, the engineers look at the software already used by the client to see whether it could be changed or if entirely new software is needed. When they have all the facts, software engineers use scientific methods and mathematical models to figure out possible solutions to

EXPLORING

- Read books about computers and careers in the field. Here are some suggestions: *Careers for Computer Buffs & Other Technological Types*, 3rd edition, by Marjorie Eberts; *The Complete Idiot's Guide to Computer Basics*, 5th edition, by Joe Kraynak; *Absolute Beginner's Guide to Computer Basics*, 5th edition, by Michael Miller; and *How Computers Work*, 9th edition, by Ron White and Timothy Edward Downs.
- Visit the Association for Computing Machinery's career Web site, http://computingcareers. acm.org, for information on career paths, a list of suggested high school classes, profiles of computer science students, and answers to frequently asked questions about the field. Another recommended site is Why Choose Computer Science & Engineering? (http://www.cs.washington.edu/WhyCSE).
- Learn as much as you can about computers, computer software, and computer hardware.
- Read computer magazines and talk to other computer users.
- Join computer clubs and search the Internet for information about working in this field.
- Try to spend a day with a working software engineer in order to experience the field firsthand. Your counselor or teacher can help you arrange such a visit.

the problems. Then they choose the best solution and prepare a written proposal for managers and other engineers.

Once a proposal is accepted, software engineers and technicians check with hardware engineers to make sure computers are powerful enough to run the new programs. The software engineers then outline program details. *Computer software engineering technicians* write the initial version in computer languages.

Throughout the programming process, engineers and technicians run diagnostic tests on the program to make sure it is working well at every stage. They also meet regularly with the client to make sure they are meeting their goals and to learn about any changes the client wants.

When a software project is complete, the engineer prepares a demonstration of it for the client. Software engineers might also install the program, train users, and be ready to help with any problems that arise in the future.

To be a successful software engineer, you should have excellent technical skills and be willing to continue to learn throughout your career. You should be a good communicator in order to work as a member of a team and interact with people who have different levels of computer knowledge. You must also be detail oriented and work well under pressure.

DID YOU KNOW?

Where Software Engineers Work

- Aerospace
- Communications
- Engineering firms
- Government/military
- Industry
- Medicine
- Science
- Software publishing

Education and Training

Take as many computer, math, and science courses as possible in high school. English and speech courses will help you improve your communication skills, which are very important for software engineers.

At least a bachelor's degree is required to work as a software engineer. A typical degree concentration for an applications software engineer is software engineering, computer science, or mathematics. Systems software engineers typically

A software engineer at NASA works on software problems that had developed with the Mars Rover. (Damian Dovarganes, AP Photo)

Profile: Anita Borg (1949–2003)

Anita Borg was a computer scientist who encouraged women to enter the male-dominated field of computer science. In 1981, she earned a Ph.D. in computer science from Courant Institute at New York University. At the time, she was one of the few women in the world with a doctorate in the field. Borg went on to have a rewarding career in research at several major computer companies.

In addition to her technical skill, Borg is perhaps best remembered for being an advocate of women in the computer industry. In 1987, she founded the Systers online community (http://anitaborg.org/initiatives/systers), where women computer professionals could network and discuss the challenges and rewards of working in the field. In 1994, she cofounded the Grace Hopper Celebration of Women in Computing (http://gracehopper.org), a series of conferences for female computer scientists. (Hopper was a famous mathematician and another groundbreaking computer scientist.) In 1997, Borg founded the Institute for Women and Technology (http://anitaborg.org).

In recognition of her work, Borg received the Augusta Ada Lovelace Award from the Association for Women in Computing; the Heinz Award for Technology, the Economy, and Employment; and numerous other awards. Borg serves as an inspiring example to young women who dream of a career in computer science.

Sources: Anita Borg Institute for Women and Technology, Association for Women in Computing

pursue a concentration in computer science or computer information systems.

Earnings

Software engineers with a bachelor's degree in computer science received average starting salaries of $61,407 in 2009, according to the National Association of Colleges and Employers. Those with bachelor's degrees in computer engineering

FOR MORE INFO

For information on careers, contact
Association for Computing Machinery
2 Penn Plaza, Suite 701
New York, NY 10121-0701
800-342-6626
acmhelp@acm.org
http://www.acm.org

For information on career opportunities
for women in computing, contact
Association for Women in Computing
41 Sutter Street, Suite 1006
San Francisco, CA 94104-4905
info@awc-hq.org
http://www.awc-hq.org

For information on computer careers and
student programs, contact
IEEE Computer Society
1730 Massachusetts Avenue, NW
Washington, DC 20036-1992

202-371-0101
http://www.computer.org

For information on certification, contact
**Institute for Certification of Computing
Professionals**
2350 East Devon Avenue, Suite 281
Des Plaines, IL 60018-4602
800-843-8227
office2@iccp.org
http://www.iccp.org

For industry information, contact
**Software & Information Industry
Association**
1090 Vermont Avenue, NW, Sixth Floor
Washington, DC 20005-4095
202-289-7442
http://www.siia.net

received $61,738. Salaries for software engineers ranged from less than $53,000 to more than $135,000 per year in 2008, according to the U.S. Department of Labor. Experienced software engineers earned more than $150,000 a year. Software engineers generally earn more in areas where there are lots of computer companies, such as California's Silicon Valley.

Outlook

Employment for software engineers is expected to be excellent during the next decade. Computer networking, the growth of the Internet and communications technology that requires software, and increasing concern about cyber security are all fueling the need for software engineers. Those with bachelor's degrees and experience in the field will have the best job prospects. Computer companies, consulting firms, major corporations, insurance agencies, banks, and countless other employers hire software engineers.

Teachers, Computer Science

What Computer Science Teachers Do

Computer science teachers help students learn how to use computers. They work in elementary school, middle school, high school, and college classrooms. Some computer science teachers may also work as adult education teachers.

Elementary and middle school computer science teachers teach basic algebraic and computer science concepts to students. *High school computer science educators* teach introductory computer science classes and more advanced classes such as computer programming, desktop publishing, web design, animation, applications (software programs such as Microsoft Word, Microsoft PowerPoint, and Corel Draw) and robotics. *College computer science educators* teach general computer science classes, as well as more specialized courses such as hardware engineering, software engineering, database management, software design, computer forensics, and computer security. They often supervise computer laboratories and serve as advisers to students.

In addition to teaching classes and supervising computer labs, computer science teachers also develop lesson plans, create and score exams, correct papers, calculate grades, and keep records. Some schools may also require teachers to lead extracurricular activities such as a computer club, competitions, and events. Teachers meet with and advise students, hold parent/teacher conferences, and attend faculty meet-

EXPLORING

- Talk to your teachers about their careers and their college experiences.
- By attending your own classes, you've already gained a good sense of the daily work of a teacher. But teachers have many duties beyond the classroom, so ask to spend some time with one of your teachers after school. Ask about her job, how she prepared for her career, and look at lecture notes and record-keeping procedures.

- Teach your younger sister or brother how to use a computer.
- Volunteer at a community center, day care center, or summer camp to get teaching experience.
- Visit the Computer Science Teachers Association's Web site, http://csta.acm.org, for a variety of career resources.
- Visit the Web sites of college computer science departments to learn more about typical classes and educators.

ings. In addition, they may have to attend local, state, and national conferences. Teachers must take continuing education courses to maintain their state's teaching license.

Teachers must be able to get along with people, have patience, and like to help others. They need good communication skills, since they may work with students from varying ethnic backgrounds and cultures. Teachers should also be well organized, as they have to keep track of the work and progress of many students. They should also be self-confident and feel comfortable in a role of authority.

An associate professor (top right) *helps a student work on a homework assignment in the Gaming Lab at Southern Polytechnic State University.* (Jason Getz, AP Photo/*Atlanta Journal-Constitution*)

Education and Training

If you want to pursue a career as a computer science teacher, you should take as many high school math and computer science courses as possible. More advanced classes such as computer programming, Web design, and animation are also beneficial. Psychology, speech, and English classes are also recommended.

DID YOU KNOW?

Where Computer Science Teachers Work

- Colleges and universities
- Community learning centers
- Elementary schools
- High schools
- Middle schools
- U.S. military

There are more than 500 accredited teacher education programs in the United States that prepare teachers for work in elementary, middle, and secondary schools. Most of these programs are designed to meet the certification requirements for the state in which they're located. Some states may require that you pass a test before being admitted to an education program. You may choose to major in computer science while taking required education courses, or you may major in education with a concentration in computer science. Although requirements for teaching licenses vary by state, all public schools require teachers to have a bachelor's degree and complete the state's approved training program.

To teach in a four-year college or university, you must have at least a master's degree. With a master's degree you can become an instructor. You will need a doctorate for a job as an assistant professor, which is the entry-level job title for college faculty. Faculty members usually spend no more than six years as assistant professors. During this time, the college will decide whether to grant you tenure, which is a type of job security, and promote you to associate professor. An associate professor may eventually be promoted to full professor.

Earnings

According to the U.S. Department of Labor, the median annual salary for secondary school teachers was $51,180 in 2008. Salaries ranged from less than $34,000 to $81,000 or more annually. The median annual salary of middle school teachers was $49,700. Those just starting out in the field earned less than $34,000. Very experienced teachers earned more than $78,000. College computer science teachers earned an average salary of $66,440 a year. Earnings ranged from less than $35,000 to $124,000 or more.

Outlook

Employment for computer science teachers is expected to be good during the next decade. Many segments of the computer industry are experiencing growth, and teachers will be need-

DID YOU KNOW?

Middle and high school students who want to become teachers can join a chapter of the Future Educators Association at their school. Member benefits include access to scholarships and a state-of-the-art social networking Web site, the chance to attend the organization's annual conference, and opportunities for hands-on career exploration opportunities. If you don't have a chapter at your school, then start one. All you need is one committed adult leader (a teacher or counselor) and at least one interested student (you, and we're sure you have a friend or two who might want to become a teacher, too). For more information, contact Future Educators Association, c/o Phi Delta Kappa International, 408 North Union Street, Bloomington, IN 47405-3800, 800-766-1156, fea@pdkintl.org, http://www.futureeducators.org.

FOR MORE INFO

To read about the issues affecting college professors, contact
American Association of University Professors
1133 Nineteenth Street, NW, Suite 200
Washington, DC 20036-3655
202-737-5900
http://www.aaup.org

For more information on becoming a teacher, contact the following organizations:
American Federation of Teachers
555 New Jersey Avenue, NW
Washington, DC 20001-2029
202-879-4400

online@aft.org
http://www.aft.org

National Education Association
1201 16th Street, NW
Washington, DC 20036-3290
202-833-4000
http://www.nea.org

For information on careers and summer programs, contact
Computer Science Teachers Association
PO Box 30778
New York, NY 10117-3509
800-342-6626
http://csta.acm.org

ed to educate the future generation of workers. The growing popularity of animated films, animated television shows, and computer and video games will also create strong demand for computer teachers with knowledge of animation techniques.

Technical Writers and Editors

What Technical Writers and Editors Do

Technical writers, also called *technical communicators*, use graphic design, page layout, and multimedia software to put scientific and technical information into language that is easily understood by the general public. They write manuals, technical reports, sales proposals, and scripts for audiovisual and video programs. Computer manuals are the most common type of manuals prepared by technical writers. The manuals that they

EXPLORING

- Try to gain experience as a writer or editor by working on a literary magazine, student newspaper, or yearbook.
- Write in a journal daily.
- Read all sorts of books, magazines, and newspapers. This will expose you to both good and bad writing and help you to identify why one approach works better than another.
- Write instructions on how to use a printer or scanner for your parents or friends. Have them follow the instructions to see if you explained the steps in the right order and with the appropriate amount of detail.
- Talk to a technical writer or editor about his or her career.

prepare tell people how to install, assemble, use, or repair computer products and other equipment. These manuals can be as simple as instructions on how to use a printer or as complex as instructions on how to build a computer system.

Technical editors work with writers to correct any errors in written material and to make text flow more clearly. They also may supervise writing projects and arrange for graphic designers, photographers, videographers, and technical illustrators to produce artwork.

Before technical writers begin writing, they gather as much information as possible about the subject. They read and review all available materials, including engineering drawings, reports, and journal articles. Technical writers interview people familiar with the topic, such as engineers, computer scientists, and computer programmers. Once they have gathered the necessary information, they write a first draft.

The writer gives copies of the rough draft to the technical editor and engineers to review. The technical editor corrects any errors in spelling, punctuation, and grammar and checks that all parts of the document are clear and easy to understand. The writer revises the rough draft based on comments from the engineers, computer scientists, programmers, and the editor. The technical editor again checks the final copy to make sure that all photos, illustrations, charts, and diagrams are properly placed, that captions match the correct pictures, and that there are no other errors.

In addition to traditional books and paper documents, technical writers and editors prepare materials for CD-ROMs, multimedia programs, e-publications, and Web sites.

At some companies, technical writers and editors have other tasks. They may work as part of a team that studies a product while it is in the early stages of development to make sure that it is well designed and easy to use. Others work with customer service or call-center managers to help analyze and improve the quality of product support services.

Education and Training

If you're interested in becoming a technical writer or editor, you should be able to understand complex, scientific ideas and explain them to others. In high school take as many English and science classes as you can. Business, journalism, math, and computer classes will also be helpful.

You will need to earn a bachelor's degree to get a job in this field. Many technical writers earn degrees in engineering or science and take technical writing classes. Technical editors may earn degrees in English, communications, or journalism. Many

Helping Hands: Michael & Susan Dell Foundation

Michael Dell is the chairman of the board of directors and chief executive officer of Dell, a computer industry leader. He founded the company in 1984 with only $1,000 and gradually turned it into one of the largest and most successful computer companies. Michael Dell is one of the richest people in the world.

Dell worked very hard to build his company into a success, but making money and selling computers wasn't enough for him. In 1999, he and his wife Susan founded the Michael & Susan Dell Foundation. It seeks to "directly improve education, health, and family economic security for children living in urban poverty around the world." It has awarded more than $530 million to help those in need. Visit http://www.msdf.org for more information about the Michael & Susan Dell Foundation.

Sources: Dell.com,
Michael & Susan Dell Foundation

technical writers and editors earn advanced degrees, such as master's degrees.

Writers and editors need to pursue learning throughout their careers to find out about the newest technologies. Experience with computer graphics and Web design is also helpful since many writers and editors prepare content for the Internet.

Many technical writers start their careers as computer scientists, engineers, programmers, or technicians and move into writing after a few years. Technical editors may start out as editorial assistants or proofreaders and advance to an editorial position once they have more experience.

> ## DID YOU KNOW?
>
> ### Where Technical Writers and Editors Work
>
> - Computer systems design industry
> - Computer and electronic manufacturing industry
> - Software publishers
> - Architectural, engineering, and related services companies
> - Management, scientific, and technical consulting services firms
> - Scientific research and development services firms
> - Colleges and universities
> - Self-employment

Earnings

Median annual earnings for salaried technical writers were $61,620 in 2008, according to the U.S. Department of Labor. Earnings for all technical writers ranged from less than $36,000 to more than $97,000. Editors earned average annual salaries of $49,990 in 2008. Those just starting out in the field earned less than $28,000. Very experienced editors made more than $95,000.

Outlook

It is hard to become a writer or editor. Each year, there are more people trying to enter this field than there are available openings. The field of technical writing and editing, though, offers more opportunities than do other areas of writing and editing, such as general-interest book publishing or journalism. Job op-

FOR MORE INFO

For information on careers, contact
Association for Computing Machinery
2 Penn Plaza, Suite 701
New York, NY 10121-0701
800-342-6626
acmhelp@acm.org
http://www.acm.org

For information on computer careers and
student programs, contact
IEEE Computer Society
1730 Massachusetts Avenue, NW
Washington, DC 20036-1992

202-371-0101
http://www.computer.org

For information on careers in technical
communication, contact
Society for Technical Communication
9401 Lee Highway, Suite 300
Arlington, VA 22203-1803
703-522-4114
stc@stc.org
http://www.stc.org

portunities for technical writers and editors are expected to be good during the next decade. Demand is growing for technical writers who can produce well-written computer manuals and other technical resources. The popularity of the Internet and the growing availability of technical materials on company Web sites will also create more opportunities for technical writers and editors.

Web Designers

What Web Designers Do

Web designers create Internet sites for small businesses, large corporations, and Internet consulting firms. They are sometimes called *Web developers, Internet developers,* or *Internet content developers.*

Web developers design Web sites and sometimes write the code that runs them. Web designers know Internet program-

EXPLORING

- Read national news magazines, newspapers, and trade magazines and surf the Web for information about Internet careers.
- Visit a variety of Web sites to study what makes them appealing or not so appealing.
- If your school has a Web site, get involved in the planning and creation of new content for it. If not, talk to your computer teachers about creating one, or create your own site at home.
- Here are some reading suggestions: *Look Mom! I Built My Own Web Site,* 2nd edition, by Zohar Amihud; *Web Design for Teens,* by Maneesh Sethi; *A Teen's Guide to Creating Web Pages and Blogs,* by Benjamin Selfridge, Peter Selfridge, and Jennifer Osburn; and *How the Internet Works,* 8th edition, by Preston Gralla.
- Talk to a Web designer about his or her career.

A Web designer (left), *senior software engineer* (center), *and vice president of engineering at a clothing company discuss a Web display.* (Kathy Willens, AP Photo)

ming languages such as Perl, Visual BASIC, CGI, Java, ActiveX, C++, Python, and HTML. Developers also know the latest graphic file formats, multimedia platforms (such as Flash), and other Web production tools.

Web designers work with companies to decide what to include or not include on their Web sites and how to present it. They consider the goals for the Web site. Some companies use the Internet simply to describe their identity, while others sell merchandise or information, present news and commentary,

Profile: Mark Zuckerberg (1984–   )

Mark Zuckerberg is the CEO of Facebook (http://www.facebook.com), the most popular social networking site on the Internet. In 2004, he cofounded Facebook while a computer science student at Harvard University. The university printed an annual directory that featured photos of students, faculty, and staff. It was known as "Facebook." Zuckerberg created an electronic version of this directory, adding user-friendly electronic features. Within a month of its founding, Zuckerberg and his cofounders (Dustin Moskov-itz, Chris Hughes, and Eduardo Saverin) expanded Facebook to be accessible to students at Stanford, Columbia, and Yale. In less than a year after its founding, Facebook had 1 million users around the country. As of December 2009, there were 350 million active Facebook users. Zuckerberg is one of the wealthiest people in the world. *Time* magazine named him one of the world's most influential people of 2008.

Source: Facebook, *Forbes, Time*

provide entertainment (including videos, animated films, photographs, blogs, or podcasts), or offer a forum for the exchange of ideas, to name a few possibilities.

Web designers also consider the potential users of the site. They try to design features that are original, that will attract attention, and that will be easy to use. A Web site can include hundreds, or even thousands, of elements, such as text, photographs, artwork, video clips, audio clips, discussion boards, credit card processing, search features, links to related Web sites, advertising banners, and animated text and graphics.

Part of the development process involves designing a general layout for the site and all its connected pages. Text is written and edited and artwork and photos are scanned and/or uploaded. All of the elements are then converted into the proper code so that they can be placed on the server. Some of this coding is now automated, but Web designers still need to monitor the automation process to ensure that everything has uploaded to the site as intended.

The career of *webmaster* is closely related to that of Web designer. While both webmasters and Web designers create and manage Web sites, webmasters typically are responsible for the more support-related duties of keeping a Web site current (such as updating text and other content, checking links for accuracy, and responding to user problems via e-mail).

Education and Training

If you are interested in this career, take as many courses as possible in computer science, science, and mathematics. These classes will give you a good foundation in computer basics and problem-solving skills. English and speech classes will improve your ability to communicate with others.

You will need a bachelor's degree in computer science or computer programming, although some designers earn degrees in noncomputer areas, such as marketing, graphic design, or information systems. Whatever degree you earn, you should have an understanding of computers and computer networks and knowledge of Internet programming languages. Further training and hands-on experience is available through internships or entry-level positions. At least one year of experience working on a Web site is a great help toward landing a job in the field.

Earnings

An entry-level position in Web development at a small company pays around $30,000. As you gain experience or move to a

FOR MORE INFO

For information on publications, contact

Association of Information Technology Professionals
401 North Michigan Avenue, Suite 2400
Chicago, IL 60611-4267
http://www.aitp.org

For information on computer careers and student programs, contact
IEEE Computer Society
1730 Massachusetts Avenue, NW
Washington, DC 20036-1992
202-371-0101
http://www.computer.org

Contact the following organizations for information on Web-based careers:

International Webmasters Association
119 East Union Street, Suite F
Pasadena, CA 91103-3952
626-449-3709
http://www.iwanet.org

World Organization of Webmasters
9580 Oak Avenue Parkway, Suite 7-177
Folsom, CA 95630-1743
916-989-2933
info@joinwow.org
http://webprofessionals.org

larger company, you might make about $60,000. The top of the pay scale is around $80,000 per year.

Outlook

The career of Web designer, like the Internet itself, is growing faster than the average. As more companies seek to attract customers on the Internet, they need developers who have the ability and expertise to create the sites to bring their products, services, and corporate images to the public and to other businesses. Web designers can expect Internet technology to continue to develop at a fast pace. This means that they will need to continue learning throughout their careers.

Webmasters

What Webmasters Do

Webmasters create and manage Web sites for large corporations, small businesses, nonprofit organizations, government agencies, schools, special interest groups, and individuals.

Some webmasters develop the content for the pages they manage. They may write the text or receive it from other writers and editors. Webmasters insert codes into the text in hypertext markup language (HTML). HTML codes tell the computer how to arrange and format the text. Webmasters also prepare images, audio, and video and add them to the Web site. They are also coded with HTML to put them in the desired size and position. (Some of this coding is now automated by computer processes, but webmasters are still needed to supervise the coding process and ensure that all items have been posted to the Web site as intended.) In addition to HTML, webmasters must be familiar with computer languages such as XML and Java, and common gateway interface (CGI) technology, which helps send Web resources to site visitors.

Many Web sites contain information that changes regularly. An organization may make changes once a day or once a week. Newspapers post updates constantly throughout the day. Webmasters maintain and update Web sites, inserting current data.

Web sites usually have links to other pages or other Web sites. Webmasters make sure the links work so that visitors to the site can connect easily to the information they need.

EXPLORING

- Spend time surfing the Web. Visit a variety of Web sites to see how they look and operate.
- Read books on Web design. Here are some reading suggestions: *Look Mom! I Built My Own Web Site,* 2nd edition, by Zohar Amihud; *Web Design for Teens,* by Maneesh Sethi; *A Teen's Guide to Creating Web Pages and Blogs,* by Benjamin Selfridge, Peter Selfridge, and Jennifer Osburn; and *How the Internet Works,* 8th edition, by Preston Gralla.
- Design your own personal Web page. Many Internet providers offer their users the option of designing and maintaining a personal Web page for a very low fee (or for free). Your Web site can contain virtually anything that you want to include—snapshots of friends, audio files of favorite music, videos, a blog, or links to your favorite sites.
- Talk to a webmaster about his or her career.

Webmasters also keep track of activity to the site. They note how often people visit their site. They answer questions and comments from visitors, usually by e-mail. Some webmasters are in charge of processing customer orders for products or services. Others create and maintain order forms or online "shopping carts" that allow visitors to the Web site to purchase products or services. Some may train other employees in how to create or update Web pages. Finally, webmasters may be responsible for developing and following a budget for their departments.

The career of *Web designer* is closely related to that of webmaster. They have many shared duties, but Web designers, as their name suggests, focus more on design-related duties.

Words to Learn

browser user-friendly software that makes Internet searches quick and efficient

Flash a multimedia platform (incorporating text, audio, video, animation, and interactivity) that has become a popular method of adding animation and interactive features to Web pages; it is also widely used for broadcast animation work

homepage a Web page that introduces the site and guides the user to other pages at the site

HTML (hypertext markup language) a code that helps control the way information on a Web page is transferred and presented and the way that hypertext links appear on the page

Internet a worldwide system of computer networks connected to each other

search engine a specialized Web site containing computer-maintained lists of other Web sites; lists are usually organized by subject, name, content, and other categories. Users request searches by typing in keywords, or topical words and phrases, and the search engine displays a list of links to related Web sites

Web page an Internet document; it is typically a hypertext document, meaning that it provides links to related Web pages, either on the same Web site or on another Web site

Web site an Internet resource that contains one or more Web pages

To be a successful webmaster, you should be creative and know what makes a Web site attractive and easy to use. You should have excellent technical ability and be willing to keep up with changing technology throughout your career. Good writing skills and an aptitude for marketing are also excellent qualities for anyone considering a career in Web site design. Other important skills for webmasters include the ability to work as a member of a team and alone, when necessary; good organizational abilities; motivation; and the ability to accept constructive criticism.

Education and Training

Take as many computer science classes as you can in high school. Many schools offer introductory courses on Web design and related topics. Math classes are also helpful. Finally, because writing skills are important in this career, English classes are a good choice.

Fame & Fortune: Larry Page and Sergey Brin

You probably don't know them by name, but one word should ring a bell: Google. Larry Page and Sergey Brin are the founders of Google, one of the most popular search engines on the Internet. The Google search engine is known for gathering fast and highly accurate search results. Google also sells software applications that can be used on computers and mobile devices such as phones, as well as advertising and other products.

Page and Brin founded Google in 1998—while they were still only in their mid-20s! The two met at Stanford University in 1995. They attended its Ph.D. program in computer science. In 1996, they began working on a search engine called BackRub. The next year, they changed the name to Google. In 1998, Page and Brin left Stanford and began developing the business, working out of a rented garage. Soon after, they incorporated their business and hired their first employee.

Page, Brin, and their employees worked day and night to make Google a success. Many people began using Google, and it became the number one search engine in 2000. Today, Google has more than 10,000 employees and offices in more than 35 countries. Page and Brin are two of the wealthiest people in the world. In creating Google, they proved that sometimes you don't have to have a lot of experience. You just have to combine great ideas with technical skill and dedication to achieve success.

Source: Google.com

A webmaster (left) *and counselor at a high school discuss new design templates for their school's Web site.* (Joe Ellis, AP Photo, *The Clarion-Ledger*)

A number of colleges and universities offer classes and certificate programs for webmasters, but there is no standard educational path or requirement for entering this field. While many webmasters have bachelor's degrees in computer science, information systems, or computer programming, liberal arts degrees such as English are not uncommon. Some webmasters also have degrees in engineering, mathematics, and marketing.

Most people who enter the field, however, do have work experience in computer technology. When considering candidates for the position of webmaster, employers usually require at least two years' experience with various Web technologies, including knowledge of HTML, JavaScript, Java, and SQL. It is quite common for someone to move into the position of webmaster from another computer-related job in the same organization.

Earnings

According to Salary.com, the average salary for webmasters in 2010 was $67,900. Salaries ranged from less than $45,000 to more than $89,000. Many webmasters, however, move into their positions from another position within their company or have webmaster duties in addition to other responsibilities. These employees tend to receive lower salaries.

Outlook

The field of computer systems design and related services is projected to be among the fastest-growing industries for the next decade. As a result, employment for webmasters is expected to be good. Many companies view Web sites as important and necessary business and marketing tools. As more and more businesses, nonprofit organizations, educational institutions, and government agencies establish Web sites or expand existing ones, there will be continued need for webmasters.

FOR MORE INFO

For information on webmaster specialties, certification, and schools that offer webmaster training, contact
International Webmasters Association
119 East Union Street, Suite F
Pasadena, CA 91103-3952
626-449-3709
http://www.iwanet.org

For education and certification information, contact
World Organization of Webmasters
9580 Oak Avenue Parkway, Suite 7-177
Folsom, CA 95630-1743
916-989-2933
info@joinwow.org
http://webprofessionals.org

Glossary

accredited   approved as meeting established standards for providing good training and education; this approval is usually given by an independent organization of professionals

annual salary   the money an individual earns for an entire year of work

apprentice   a person who is learning a trade by working under the supervision of a skilled worker; apprentices often receive classroom instruction in addition to their supervised practical experience

associate's degree   an academic rank or title granted by a community college, junior college, or similar institution to graduates of a two-year program of education beyond high school

bachelor's degree   an academic rank or title given to a person who has completed a four-year program of study at a college or university; also called an undergraduate degree or baccalaureate

career   an occupation for which a worker receives training and has an opportunity for advancement

certified   approved as meeting established requirements for skill, knowledge, and experience in a particular field; people are certified by an organization of professionals in their field

college   an educational institution that is above the high school level

community college   a public or private two-year college attended by students who do not usually live at the college; graduates of a community college receive an associate's degree and may transfer to a four-year college or university to complete a bachelor's degree

diploma   a certificate or document given by a school to show that a person has completed a course or has graduated from the school

distance education   a type of educational program that allows students to take classes and complete their education by mail or the Internet

doctorate   the highest academic rank or title granted by a graduate school to a person who has completed a two- to three-year program after having received a master's degree

fellowship   a financial award given for research projects or dissertation assistance; fellowships are commonly offered at the graduate, postgraduate, or doctoral levels

freelancer   a worker who is not a regular employee of a company; freelancers contract with companies for specific work or projects and receive payment that is not considered wages

fringe benefit   a payment or benefit to an employee in addition to regular wages or salary; examples of fringe benefits include a pension, a paid vacation, and health or life insurance

graduate school   a school that people may attend after they have received their bachelor's degree; people who complete an educational program at a graduate school earn a master's degree or a doctorate

intern   an advanced student (usually one with at least some college training) in a professional field who is employed in a job that is intended to provide supervised practical experience for the student

internship   the position or job of an intern; also, the period of time when a person is an intern

junior college   a two-year college that offers courses like those in the first half of a four-year college program; graduates of a junior college usually receive an associate's degree and may transfer to a four-year college or university to complete a bachelor's degree

liberal arts   the subjects covered by college courses that develop broad general knowledge rather than specific occupational skills; the liberal arts are often considered to include philosophy, literature, the arts, history, language, and some courses in the social sciences and natural sciences

major (in college)   the academic field in which a student specializes and receives a degree

master's degree   an academic rank or title granted by a graduate school to a person who has completed a one- or two-year program after having received a bachelor's degree

medical degree   a degree awarded to an individual who has completed four years of training at a medical school

pension   an amount of money paid regularly by an employer to a former employee after he or she retires from working

scholarship   a gift of money to a student to help the student pay for further education

social studies   courses of study (such as civics, geography, and history) that deal with how human societies work

starting salary   salary paid to a newly hired employee; the starting salary is usually a smaller amount than is paid to a more experienced worker

technical college   a private or public college offering two- or four-year programs in technical subjects; technical colleges offer courses in both general and technical subjects and award associate's degrees and bachelor's degrees

undergraduate   a student at a college or university who has not yet received a degree

undergraduate degree   see **bachelor's degree**

union   an organization of workers in a particular industry or company; the union works to gain better wages, benefits, and working conditions for its members; also called a labor union or trade union

vocational school   a public or private school that offers training in one or more skills or trades

wage   money that is paid in return for work done, especially money paid on the basis of the number of hours or days worked

Browse and Learn More

Books

Amihud, Zohar. *Look Mom! I Built My Own Web Site.* 2d ed. Fords, N.J.: BookChamp, 2006.

Burnett, Rebecca. *Careers for Number Crunchers & Other Quantitative Types.* 2d ed. New York: McGraw-Hill, 2002.

Clemens, Meg, Glenn Clemens, and Sean Clemens. *The Everything Kids' Math Puzzles Book: Brain Teasers, Games, and Activities for Hours of Fun.* Cincinnati, Ohio: Adams Media Corporation, 2003.

Costanza, Marcelle. *Creative Computer Crafts: 50 Fun and Useful Products You Can Make with Any Inkjet Printer.* San Francisco: No Starch Press, 2006.

Darby, Jason. *Game Creation for Teens.* Florence, Ky.: Course Technology PTR, 2008.

Derfler, Frank, Jr. *How Networks Work.* 7th ed. Indianapolis, Ind.: Que Publishing, 2004.

Eberts, Marjorie. *Careers for Computer Buffs & Other Technological Types.* 3d ed. New York: McGraw-Hill, 2006.

Edelfelt, Roy, and Alan Reiman. *Careers in Education.* 4th ed. New York: McGraw-Hill, 2003.

Fine, Janet. *Opportunities in Teaching Careers.* New York: McGraw-Hill, 2005.

Fisher, Ian K. *How to Start a Career in Information Technology.* 2d ed. New York: Ian K. Fisher, 2007.

Gralla, Preston. *How the Internet Works.* 8th ed. Indianapolis, Ind.: Que Publishing, 2006.

Harbour, Jonathan S. *Visual Basic Game Programming for Teens.* Florence, Ky.: Course Technology PTR, 2004.

Kraynak, Joe. *The Complete Idiot's Guide to Computer Basics.* 5th ed. New York: Alpha, 2009.

Miller, Michael. *Absolute Beginner's Guide to Computer Basics.* 5th ed. Indianapolis, Ind.: Que Publishing, 2009.

Pardew, Les. *Game Art for Teens.* 2d ed. Florence, Ky.: Course Technology PTR, 2005.

Pardew, Les. *Game Design for Teens.* Florence, Ky.: Course Technology PTR, 2004.

Peterson's. *Peterson's Summer Opportunities for Kids & Teenagers.* 26th ed. Lawrenceville, N.J.: Peterson's, 2008.

Rathbone, Andy. *Upgrading & Fixing PCs For Dummies.* 7th ed. Hoboken, N.J.: For Dummies, 2007.

Romano, Amy. *Cool Careers without College for People Who Love Everything Digital.* New York: Rosen Publishing Group, 2007.

Sande, Warren, and Carter Sande. *Hello World!: Computer Programming for Kids and Other Beginners.* Greenwich, Conn.: Manning Publications, 2009.

Selfridge, Benjamin, Peter Selfridge, and Jennifer Osburn. *A Teen's Guide to Creating Web Pages and Blogs.* Waco, Tex.: Prufrock Press, 2008.

Sethi, Maneesh. *Game Programming for Teens.* 3d ed. Florence, Ky.: Course Technology PTR, 2008.

Sethi, Maneesh. *Web Design for Teens.* Florence, Ky.: Course Technology PTR, 2004.

Sterrett, Andrew, ed. *101 Careers in Mathematics.* 2d ed. Washington, D.C.: Mathematical Association of America, 2003.

Takahashi, Mana. *The Manga Guide to Databases.* San Francisco: No Starch Press, 2008.

White, Ron, and Timothy Edward Downs. *How Computers Work.* 9th ed. Indianapolis, Ind.: Que Publishing, 2007.

Periodicals

Computer Graphics World
http://www.cgw.com

eGFI: Dream Up the Future
http://www.egfi-k12.org/read-the-magazine

Game Developer
http://www.gdmag.com

Information Security
http://www.infosecuritymag.com

The Pre-Engineering Times
http://www.jets.org/publications/petimes.cfm

Web Sites

American Federation of Teachers: Becoming a Teacher
http://www.aft.org/pdfs/tools4teachers/becomingateacher0608.pdf

American Library Association: Great Web Sites for Kids
http://www.ala.org/greatsites

Breaking In: Preparing for Your Career in Games
http://archives.igda.org/breakingin

Building a School Website
http://www.wigglebits.com

Computer History Museum
http://www.computerhistory.org

Computing Degrees and Careers
http://computingcareers.acm.org

CoolMath.com
http://coolmath.com

eGFI: Dream Up the Future
http://egfi-k12.org

Finding Data on the Internet
http://www.robertniles.com/data

Free On-Line Dictionary of Computing
http://foldoc.org

Hobbes Internet Timeline
http://www.zakon.org/robert/internet/timeline

Invention Dimension
http://web.mit.edu/invent/invent-main.html

Math Cats
http://www.mathcats.com

Math Playground
http://www.MathPlayground.com

National Inventors Hall of Fame
http://www.invent.org/hall_of_fame/1_0_0_hall_of_fame.asp

Sloan Career Cornerstone Center
http://careercornerstone.org

The Tech Museum of Innovation
http://www.thetech.org

Why Choose Computer Science & Engineering?
http://www.cs.washington.edu/WhyCSE

Index